TODAY,
LORD, I WILL

A Daily Devotional

TODAY, LORD, I WILL

AL BRYANT

WORD BOOKS
PUBLISHER
WACO, TEXAS

Library of Congress Cataloging in Publication Data:
  Bryant, Al, 1926-
    Today, Lord, I Will.

    Includes indexes.
    I. Devotional calendars. I. Title.
  BV4811.B78 1982   242'.2   82-50510
  ISBN 0-8499-0321-1

Unless otherwise indicated, Scripture quotations are from
The King James Version of the Bible.

Other Scripture quotations in this publication are from
the following sources:
    The Revised Standard Version of the Bible (RSV), copyright © 1946,
1952, © 1971 and 1973 by the Division of Christian Education of the
National Council of the Churches of Christ in the U.S.A.
    The Living Bible, Paraphrased (TLB), copyright © 1971 by Tyndale
House Publishers, Wheaton, Illinois.
    The New International Version of the Bible (NIV), published by The
Zondervan Corporation, copyright © 1978 by the New York International
Bible Society.
    The Modern Language Bible: The New Berkeley Version in Modern English.
Copyright © 1945, 1959, 1969 by Zondervan Publishing House.
    The Amplified New Testament (AB), © The Lockman Foundation 1954, 1958.

To my granddaughter

JESSICA RENÉE BRYANT

who brightens my life
and lengthens my love

Foreword

Today, Lord, I Will is a book that dares to be different. I have compiled, written, read, and enjoyed devotional books for many years—and they all had one thing in common: a passive acceptance of sometimes towering truths without any opportunity or incentive to get out and *do* something with what I had learned. They offered inspiration but no possibility of perspiration. This, it seemed to me, was in some ways a weakness in this honored and well-loved genre of Christian literature. And I set out to *do* something about it in this book.

Today, Lord, I Will offers the reader brief, brisk, pithy meditations on a whole multitude of subjects with one underlying similarity: all are dealing with practical spiritual concerns or issues. Each one is solidly based in the scripture reference quoted at the beginning of the page, but a broader section of Scripture is suggested for background reading for those who prefer a stronger emphasis on biblical content in their devotional exercises.

Then, to encourage what I call "do-it-yourself devotions," at the end of the intensely personal and introspective meditations herein are groups of two or more questions "for further thought." Below that appears space for writing-in your own personal thoughts and goals for that day based on what you have just read and experienced. I suggest a way to begin your "diary" entry, but feel free to ignore my suggestion in favor of your own inclination. It is my prayer that this book will start a whole new emphasis in devotional reading—an emphasis on doing as well as experiencing.

Several indexes are provided at the end of this volume to make its contents more accessible to you. A subject index will help you find meditations dealing with particular subject areas. An index of persons and periodicals quoted will supply that information. In addition, a scripture index and an index of scripture readings has been supplied.

This book differs from my previous devotional books in another area as well. *Climbing the Heights, Climbing Higher,* and *LoveSongs* were envisioned as books to be read together—either in a group or with one's spouse. This book, however, is designed to be read by you *personally*. In fact, it is my hope that when you have completed your journal for the year, it will be as long or longer than the already suggested devotional thoughts. Your personal written-in comments on the Scripture passages should end up meaning more to you than mine! If that happens, the book will have been successful in achieving its goal to involve you personally in the adventure of living each day to its fullest.

AL BRYANT

March 1982

And he led them forth by the right way, that they might go to a city of habitation.

—Psalm 107:7

Nothing is more important at the beginning of a journey than that we should make a right start. To be in the right way we must follow the right Guide. It is not written, "They went in the right way," but "*He* led them." They could never have found it, much less continued in it, without the Lord's leading. The right way is always his way. And that is more than just an abstract concept; "the right way" means the right way for me—what God is leading me to do today, in my daily life. "Show me thy ways, O Lord" (Ps. 25:4).

We sometimes fail to know and follow God's guidance, because we allow too great a space to come between us and him. The beginning of a new year is a good time to draw close to our Guide, to seek the guidance that keeps us not only safe, but happy and blessed.

With David I pray: "Good and upright is the Lord; therefore he instructs sinners in the way. He leads the humble in what is right, and teaches the humble his way" (Ps. 25:8, 9, RSV). Lord, keep me humble and teachable through this coming year!

For further consideration:
1. Am I really willing to be led by God?
2. How will seeking his guidance for "the right way" affect how I plan today's schedule?

Today, Lord, I will:

2 JANUARY

Let us go forth therefore unto him without the camp, bearing his reproach. For here we have no continuing city, but we seek one to come.

—Hebrews 13:13, 14

Identification with Christ has two sides—before God, and before men. In the first, we find the secret of life and joy and liberty. In the second, we must expect to meet with rejection, reproach, and shame. If we glory in the fact that we are one with him in his death, his resurrection and exaltation, let us not shrink from taking our right place with him as "the despised and rejected of men." "Let us go forth unto him without the camp." This implies something more than a mere passive contemplation: it means an active consecration. What is Christ's reproach? It does not mean being opposed and rejected merely; it means being *despised*. There is nothing men shrink from as from this. It is easier to endure open opposition than to be ignored and despised. "Here we have no continuing city, but we seek one to come." Here we are strangers and pilgrims. This is only for a while. Soon we shall see the Eternal City. There we shall share with him the glory and the honor.

EVAN HOPKINS

For further thought:
1. How am I living my life here on earth—as if this were all there is?
2. What are some of the ways those around me can make me feel "despised" because of my Christian beliefs?

In search of inner strength, today I will:

And the second is like unto it, Thou shalt love thy neighbor as thyself.
                                                            —Matthew 22:39

What is meant by our neighbor we cannot doubt: it is everyone with whom we are brought into contact! First of all, he is literally our neighbor who is next to us in our own family and household: husband to wife, wife to husband, parent to child, brother to sister, master to servant, servant to master. Then it is he who is close to us in our own neighborhood, in our own town, in our own parish, in our own street. With these all true charity begins. To love and be kind to these is the very beginning of all true religion. But, besides these, as our Lord teaches, it is every one who is thrown across our path by the changes and chances of life; he or she, whoever it be, whom we have any means of helping—the unfortunate stranger whom we may meet in traveling, the deserted friend whom no one else cares to look after.

                                        A. P. STANLEY (1815–1882)

For further thought:
1. Is this passage pointing me to any particular "neighbor"?
2. Have I "missed" helping a neighbor whom I should have touched recently?

To better love my neighbor, today I will:

4 JANUARY

And this is love, that we follow his commandments; this is the commandment, as you heard from the beginning, that you follow love.
—2 John 6, RSV

This passage really speaks to me in the area of obedience and loving my neighbor. So often I get "the cart before the horse." I ask the Lord to use me, forgetting to pray that I might be, first of all, in the center of his will, right where he wants me to be. If I could only learn that following his commandments, living according to his plan for my life, will automatically put me in the place of loving my neighbor as I should. Love requires that I place the needs of others before my own selfish concerns. By so doing I can give God his proper place in my life—and live out the command that I follow love.

For further thought:

1. Is there someone in my life right now whom I am simply to "love" and let God do the rest?
2. Am I "abiding" as I should in the "doctrine of Christ"?

Today, Lord, I will:

For I have come down from heaven, not to do my own will, but the will of him who sent me.

—John 6:38, RSV

Jesus had discovered the real secret of soul satisfaction—complete surrender to the Father's will. Because he rested completely in that commitment, he lived with a serenity that drew others to him. J. Hudson Taylor (1832–1905), intrepid pioneer missionary to China and founder of the vast China Inland Mission, had this observation: "The real secret of an unsatisfied life lies too often in an unsurrendered will." When I encounter problems in my Christian life, I can usually trace them to a failure to submit my will to my heavenly Father. This is the reason for my discontent and dissatisfaction. So often I sacrifice the eternal on the altar of the immediate, because my will is not conformed to my Father's. If only I could learn, once and for all, the secret of serenity and live my life in the attitude of surrender that Jesus modeled when he was here on earth!

For further thought:
1. Why is it that only certain Christians seem to learn the secret of surrender?
2. What specific aspects of my life do I need to surrender to Jesus right now?

O Lord, help me to:

6 JANUARY

Read Matthew 8:23–27

And he said to them, "Why are you afraid, O men of little faith?"
Then he rose and rebuked the winds and the sea; and there was a
great calm.

—Matthew 8:26, RSV

I never cease to be amazed at how the Scriptures dovetail from beginning to end. For example, Jesus' action described here by Matthew had been minutely foretold in the Psalms, first by David: "O God of our salvation... who dost still the roaring of the seas, the roaring of their waves, the tumult of the peoples?" (65:5–7, RSV). In Psalm 89:9 and 107:29 the message comes again: "Thou dost rule the raging of the sea; when its waves arise, thou stillest them.... He made the storm be still, and the waves of the sea were hushed" (RSV). Henry Drummond (1851–1897), Scottish writer and evangelist, said: "Christ's life outwardly was one of the most troubled lives that was ever lived—tempest and tumult, tumult and tempest, the waves breaking over it all the time till the worn body was laid in the grave. But the inner life was a sea of glass. The great calm was always there. At any moment, you might have gone to Him and found rest."

For further thought:
1. What tumult in my life needs calming?
2. Have I ever allowed Jesus to instill peace in my life?

Today I will let God's peace:

JANUARY 7

Acquaint now thyself with him, and be at peace.

—Job 22:21

I like the way the Revised Standard Version reads here: "*Agree with God, and be at peace.*" *The Living Bible* is even stronger: "Quit quarrelling with God! Agree with him and you will have peace at last! His favor will surround you if you will only admit that you were wrong." Peace is possible only in a right relationship with God. I like to think of God as standing with his hand outstretched to me, just waiting for me to extend mine to him so that we can come into fellowship and I can be drawn ever closer to him. Before this can happen I have to make myself completely vulnerable to him. My life has to be an open book, with every page available for his perusal. Anything held back will hinder my peace.

To think about:

1. What is there in my life that keeps me from being "acquainted" with God?
2. Is there anyone other than God with whom I can be completely open and vulnerable?

I want peace for my portion today, so I will:

8 JANUARY

Read 1 John 3:1–10

How great is the love the Father has lavished upon us, that we should be called children of God! And that is what we are! ...
—1 John 3:1, NIV

The King James Version reads, "Behold, what manner of love the Father hath bestowed upon us, that we should be called the sons of God." What kind of love was the Father's love? We bandy the word "love" about today without much of a concept of what true love really is! The original Greek has many different words for "love"; the one used here is *agape*. Most earthly love comes in response to love offered to us, it's "because of" love. But God's love—*agape* love—is "in spite of" love. He loves us not because of who we are but because of who *he* is. He then calls upon us to reflect this unselfish, other-centered love to all those around us— not because they deserve it but because he commands it and empowers us to do it.

For further thought:

1. In what ways have I felt God's *agape* love acting in my life?
2. Can I show love that consistently? If I live and love this way, am I going to be considered an oddball?

To show God's love today I will:

Therefore I tell you, do not worry about your life, what you will eat or drink; or about your body, what you will wear. Is not life more important than food, and the body more important than clothes?
—Matthew 6:25, NIV

The Christian life has a practical dimension that I don't often think about. My heavenly Father is as concerned for my physical welfare as he is about my spiritual well-being. The cost of just "getting along" in our inflated economy is constantly increasing, and sometimes I can't help wondering where it will all lead. The demands made upon me drain my energy and sap my strength. To whom shall I go when I'm concerned about my physical needs? The same One to whom I go with my spiritual needs. He's just as available to meet the mundane as he is to deal with massive and momentous problems. Lord, let me live my life joyously, knowing that you care and are there!

For further consideration:
1. In what ways have I compartmentalized my life—offering God the spiritual but not the physical?
2. What are some material concerns in my life I need to turn over to God?

I want to live joyously today, so I will:

Who of you by worrying can add a single hour to his life?
—Matthew 6:27, NIV

How foolish it is for me to worry and fret! An hour of anxiety cannot change my circumstances, but a minute of prayer can alter everything! Paul says, "Have no anxiety about anything, but in everything by prayer and supplication with thanksgiving let your requests be made known to God. And the peace of God, which passes all understanding, will keep your hearts and your minds in Christ Jesus" (Phil. 4:6, 7, RSV). If I really lived as though I believe that (and the Bible is full of such promises), I wouldn't get "uptight" about the daily pressures on me, the demands that sometimes drain me.

To think about:
1. What could I do to make my Christianity more practical?
2. How could I adjust my schedule to make room in my life for "the peace of God"?
3. What kind of things do I worry about? How would I be different if I really learned what the Bible tells me about worry and anxiety?

To put his peace into practice, today I will:

Devote yourselves to prayer, being watchful and thankful.
—Colossians 4:2, NIV

The Living Bible emphasizes a different aspect of this verse: "Don't be weary in prayer; keep at it; watch for God's answers and be thankful when they come." The Christian life is dependent upon constant communication. Just as Jesus was in continual and constant touch with his heavenly Father, I need to maintain a constant "open line" to heaven. And there's more involved than continual "asking"—I'm to be careful and consistent in thanksgiving as well. That means *listening* as well as *talking*—resting as well as walking. Once I've learned to turn my weariness over to the Great Burden-bearer, I should be more effective in both talking and walking.

For further contemplation:
1. Am I involved in "two-way" prayer?
2. Am I as consistent in *thanking* God as I am in *asking* him?
3. If every Christian had a prayer life like mine, what kind of church would we have?

Since prayer is so important in the Christian life, today I will:

And pray in the Spirit on all occasions with all kinds of prayers and requests. With this in mind, be alert and always keep on praying for all the saints.

—Ephesians 6:18, NIV

It almost seems that these words could have been a part of the Colossians passage which was yesterday's text—and this reminds me of the fact that the people to whom Paul wrote in both Colossae and Ephesus were *real people.* That's why Paul's writings in particular, and the Bible in general, are so practical and applicable to life situations in every century and culture. *Sunshine* magazine once carried the little line: "Don't expect a thousand-dollar answer to a ten-cent prayer." I suppose this could be paraphrased for our inflationary times, "Don't expect a million-dollar answer to a ten dollar prayer"—but the truth is still the same. Praying is serious business—and it shouldn't be entered into lightly. Lord, help me to remember that.

To think about:
1. What kinds of prayers do I pray?
2. Am I serious about prayer—or do I just go through motions, expecting nothing?
3. Are my prayers self-centered or other-centered?

Beginning today, I'm going to pray for:

But whatever happens to me [Paul], remember always to live as Christians should, so that, whether I ever see you again or not, I will keep on hearing good reports that you are standing side by side with one strong purpose—to tell the Good News.

—Philippians 1:27, LB

Our business in life is not to get ahead of other people, but to get ahead of ourselves. To break our own record; to outstrip our yesterdays by todays; to bear our trials more beautifully than we ever dreamed we could; to whip the tempter inside and out as we never whipped him before; to give as we never have given; to do our work with more force and a finer finish than ever; to get ahead of ourselves—that is the true idea. To beat someone else in a game, or to be beaten, may mean much or little. To beat ourselves means a great deal. Whether we win or not, we are playing better than we ever did before, and that's the point after all—to play better the game of life.

M. D. BABCOCK (1858–1901)

For further thought:
1. What is the "strong purpose" in my life? Have I let myself drift along without developing clear-cut goals and purposes?
2. When is ambition wrong, and when is it a healthy drive to move forward?

In the light of my "strong purpose," Lord, today I will strive to:

14 JANUARY

Then flew one of the seraphim to me, having in his hand a burning coal which he had taken with tongs from the altar. And he touched my mouth and said: "Behold this has touched your lips; your guilt is taken away, and your sin forgiven."

—Isaiah 6:6, RSV

Touching God is like touching a live wire. He sends his power through me like a bolt of lightning. A person can touch a dead wire and not be changed—or not even know he touched it. It is impossible to touch God and not be moved. However, we cry as did Isaiah of old, "Woe is me! For I am lost... for my eyes have seen the King, the Lord of hosts" (6:5, RSV). But touching God can be a gentle, calming experience as well. To meet God this way in the morning assures me a day of compassionate service to others. I need more of God in my life, more of his purity, love, grace, and strength. If all spiritual help comes from him, if he is the source and substance of all blessing and benediction, then my first and foremost care ought to be to meet him alone in the morning hour.

For further thought:
1. How long has it been since God has touched me—or I have touched God?
2. Is there a better time for me than the morning for these moments with him?

O Lord, help me today to let you touch me in the following ways:

By faith Abraham, when he was tried, offered up Isaac: and he that had received the promises offered up his only begotten son.
—Hebrews 11:17

It wasn't so much the *quantity* of Abraham's faith as the *quality* of that trust which is pictured here in Hebrews. Because Abraham was a rich man, he could have sacrificed an animal and never missed the cost of such an offering. But God demanded a deeper faith than that, and asked for Isaac, Abraham's only son—foreshadowing the price paid by God for mankind's sin, *His* only Son!

God asks for my very best—my choicest possession. Edward Young, eighteenth century poet, clarifies it for me: "Faith is not only a means of obeying, but a principal act of obedience; not only an altar on which to sacrifice, but a sacrifice itself, and perhaps, of all, the greatest. It is the submission of our understandings; an oblation of our idolized reason to God, which he requires so indispensably, that our whole will and affections, though seemingly a larger sacrifice, will not, without it, be received at his hands." If I give him but a measure of myself, I might as well not give at all.

For further thought:
1. What is my "best" which needs to be given to God?
2. Is there a part of my life I am knowingly withholding from him right now?

In submission to God today, I will:

16 JANUARY

I will sing about your lovingkindness and your justice, Lord. I will sing your praises.

—Psalm 101:1, LB

Scientists tell of certain birds which in their wild state do not sing, but which have in their throats fine muscles, showing that if they had grown up in a favorable environment they might have been good singers. There is not one who has not more life muscles than he has learned to use. We have capacities for obedience, for service, for beautiful living, for usefulness which lie undeveloped in us. Instead of letting ourselves slacken in the doing of our duty, we should ever set ourselves a higher work, and every day add a line to the quality of our life and the worthiness of our character.

J. R. MILLER (1840–1912)

For further thought:
1. What gifts have I discovered in my life that I could be using for God?
2. Am I aware of any gifts that I am not using for God?
3. Am I "coasting" spiritually?

O Lord, help me today to:

The Lord is my Shepherd; I shall not want.

—Psalm 23:1

   The Living Bible translates this verse: "Because the Lord is my Shepherd, I have everything I need!" I like that, for it has a ring of reality and victory that should characterize the Christian's attitude toward his circumstances. We may not have everything we "want," but our Shepherd certainly sees to it that we have everything we "need!" Sometimes we need the discipline of difficulty which Paul talked about and called his "thorn in the flesh." Driven beyond our own resources, we learn what it really means to fall back upon the inexhaustible riches of our great Savior.

For further contemplation:
1. How long is my life here on earth in comparison to what's ahead?
2. What "discipline" is there in my life, and how am I reacting to it?
3. Does my prayer life reveal any "wants" that aren't *needs*?

As I kneel in prayer today, I will ask for:

18 JANUARY

Because of the Lord's great love we are not consumed, for his compassions never fail. They are new every morning; great is your faithfulness.

—Lamentations 3:22, 23, NIV

What a contrast there is between the "compassion" of men and the love of God, our heavenly Father and Great Shepherd. *The Living Bible* reads, "His compassion never ends. It is only the Lord's great mercies that have kept us from complete destruction." Men are here today and gone tomorrow, so far as their compassion is concerned. They can care deeply about someone or something today—and move on to new areas of concern tomorrow without a backward look. Not so our God. "His compassion never ends." He goes every step of the way, every hour of the day, with me. That's why I have everything I need!

Something to think about:
1. Am I living my life in the light of this great promise?
2. Do I really *believe* that "his compassion never ends"? If I did, would I live my life any differently?

In the light of God's compassion, I will:

JANUARY 19

When they looked up, they saw no one except Jesus.
—Matthew 17:8, NIV

There is a tremendous spiritual lesson wrapped up in these ten words. Notice the direction Jesus' disciples looked—up! Notice the object of their attention—Jesus! Notice the centrality of their concentration—they saw Jesus only! The lesson we need to learn is to *keep* our eyes on Jesus. If we look to men around us for inspiration or fellowship, sooner or later we are bound to be discouraged and disillusioned, for men are fallible, human creatures at best. It is inevitable that they will stumble or fall, and our ideal of them will invariably be shattered. But Jesus is perfect and imperishable. We will never be disappointed in him. O Lord, let me see "no one except Jesus"!

For further thought:

1. Is there someone in my life who has the place of prominence Jesus should have?
2. Is "seeing Jesus only" a narrow thought? Is a "Jesus only" life too restricted for this modern day?

Today I will see "Jesus only" by:

I will say this: because these experiences I had were so tremendous, God was afraid I might be puffed up by them; so I was given a physical condition which has been a thorn in my flesh, a messenger from Satan to hurt and bother me, and prick my pride.

—2 Corinthians 12:7, LB

There is a "ministry of suffering." Paul experienced it—and Christians down through the ages have learned in the "school of hard knocks." Out of pain can come beauty. The beautiful rose is surrounded by thorns. The mountain flower struggles up through the winter snow to be kissed by the spring sun. So we as Christians should be thankful for thorns. The beauty of holiness is not lightly won. As Paul says elsewhere, "When I am weak, then I am strong." Only God can bring strength out of struggle, peace out of pain. Thorns in the flesh can take many forms—but if they come from God, they have a purpose!

Things to think about:
1. Do I have a "thorn in the flesh"? Might it have been given to "prick my pride"?
2. How can a "thorn" come both from Satan and my Savior?

My "thorn in the flesh" is:

As I trust God to bring beauty out of my suffering, today I will:

Then the angel of God, who had been traveling in front of Israel's army, withdrew and went behind them. The pillar of cloud also moved from in front and stood behind them, coming between the armies of Egypt and Israel.

—Exodus 14:19, 20, NIV

This whole episode offers a prime spiritual lesson if we will take the time to discern it. J. R. Miller (1840–1912) gives this explanation: "It is not always guidance that we most need. Many of our dangers come upon us from behind . . . assaulting us when we are unaware of their nearness. The tempter is cunning and shrewd. He does not (always) meet us full front. It is a comfort to know that Christ comes behind us when it is there we need the protection."

No question about it—there *are* times when I need protection from the tempter rather than guidance—and my God is equal to my need! Whether I need guidance *or* protection—and when I need both at once—my Savior stands ready. If it's protection I need, he surrounds me with his care, before and behind. If it's guidance I need, he goes before in the pillar of cloud. It is my place to be where he can guide and protect me—in the center of his will!

For further thought:
1. From what in my life right now do I need protection?
2. What specific guidance do I need at this moment?

O Lord, I thank you for both protection and guidance. Today I will:

22 JANUARY

Not that we are sufficient of ourselves to think any thing as of ourselves; but our sufficiency is from God.

—2 Corinthians 3:5

R. A. Torrey (1856–1928), American evangelist and Bible scholar, explained it this way: "As far as we are told in the Bible, the Holy Spirit has no way of getting at the unsaved except through the channel of those who are already saved; He comes to the believer and through the believer convinces the unsaved of sin. What a solemn thought! If we realized that the Holy Spirit could only reach the unbeliever through us, who are already saved, would we not be more careful to present an unchoked channel through which the Spirit of God could work?" Mine is a solemn responsibility—but God is sufficient for all my needs. He doesn't demand without offering the strength to carry out the task assigned.

For further thought:
1. Is there some person to whom I am to witness today?
2. Have I passed up an opportunity I should have taken?
3. Is there anything in my life "choking" my channel?

Today I will:

Read 2 Peter 3:8–13
See Psalm 90:4

JANUARY 23

Be not ignorant of this one thing, that one day is with the Lord as a thousand years, and a thousand years as one day.

—2 Peter 3:8

I believe that if we could only see beforehand what it is that our heavenly Father means us to be—the *soul* beauty and perfection and glory, the glorious and lovely spiritual body that this soul is to dwell in through all eternity—if we could have a glimpse of *this*, we should not grudge all the trouble and pains he is taking with us now, to bring us up to that ideal which is his thought of us. We know that it is God's way to work slowly, so we must not be surprised if he takes a great many years of discipline to turn a mortal being into an immortal, glorious angel.

ANNIE KEARY (1825–1879)

For further thought:

1. Have there been times in the past when I have become impatient with God, only to discover the wisdom of his timing?
2. In what sense does God have an overview of my life?

In the light of God's overarching view of my life, today I will:

On the day of judgment men will render account for every careless word they utter; for by your words you will be justified, and by your words you will be condemned.

—Matthew 12:36, 37, RSV

Jesus was speaking strong words to the hypocritical Pharisees here—but this passage contains a lesson for us as well. Words reveal the inward attitudes of the heart just as surely as do actions (see 2 Cor. 5:10). And the Lord can see into our hearts even more clearly than can today's electrocardiogram. So dependable is this divine scanner that its evidence will stand up in court—one can be "justified" or "condemned" by its expert testimony. I wonder what my words and actions reveal about my lifestyle. Am I "careless" in the way I carry out my spiritual responsibilities? Whatever I'm doing, in a sense I'm on trial. What will God's verdict be?

For further thought:
1. What would I be ashamed for others to know about me?
2. Do I live daily as if God's x-ray vision were trained on me?

Today I will:

JANUARY 25

Be not ye therefore like unto them; for your father knoweth what things ye have need of, before ye ask him.

—Matthew 6:8

Lord, I know not what I ought to ask of Thee; Thou only knowest what I need; Thou lovest me better than I know how to love myself. O Father! Give to Thy child that which he himself knows not how to ask. I dare not ask either for crosses or consolations; I simply present myself before Thee; I open my heart to Thee. Behold my needs which I know not myself; see, and do according to Thy tender mercy. Smite, or heal; depress me, or raise me up; I adore all Thy purposes without knowing them; I am silent; I offer myself in sacrifice; I yield myself to Thee; I would have no other desire than to accomplish Thy will. Teach me to pray; pray Thyself in me.

FRANCOIS DE LA MOTHE FENELON (1808–1892)

For further thought:
1. Can I pray a prayer like this from my heart?
2. When is the last time I've experienced an answer to prayer?
3. Have there ever been times when God has filled a need I didn't even know I had?

Lord, I believe in prayer, and today I ask you to:

Things began to happen before he had done speaking [in prayer to God]....

—Genesis 24:15, MLB

Here's a remarkable lesson in answered prayer. Even before Abraham's obedient servant completed his prayer for guidance in securing a wife for Isaac, "Things began to happen...." That's the way God answers the believer's prayer. And that's why prayer should have such a major place in my daily life. Whatever my need—guidance in finding a mate, wisdom in handling a domestic crisis, understanding in a delicate interpersonal relationship, insight in making a difficult decision—God has the resources to lead me in the right way or to the right person, just as he did this humble servant of Abraham. If I will pray honestly and openly, sharing my need, he can meet my need even before the words leave my mouth!

For further thought:

1. Do I pray as specifically as did this servant?
2. If I don't, is that perhaps why my prayers are not answered as promptly and precisely as his was?

Lord, today I pray that you will:

JANUARY 27

Forever, O Lord, thy word is settled in heaven.

—Psalm 119:89

A popular gospel song, speaking of the Lord, says, "He never changes!" And another Scripture verse says, "Jesus Christ the same yesterday, and today, and for ever" (Heb. 13:8). Jesus is the Living Word. And he is also the One who stands behind and permeates the other Word of God—this Bible that I revere, but also, unfortunately, neglect and even take for granted. To think that the One who made the world and has complete authority over it is the same One who accompanies me on my daily path! This is a concept I cannot grasp, so vast and awesome is it in its implications. What a foundation of faithfulness it offers me to stand upon! With Martin Luther I must confess, "Here I stand! I can do no other!"

Things to think about:

1. My heavenly Father's authority is absolute—but is my obedience unquestioning?
2. What does it mean to have a solid foundation on which to stand—or build?
3. How should my relationship with the Word make a difference in my life?

With the Word of the Lord as my foundation, today I will:

28 JANUARY

Thy word have I hid in mine heart, that I might not sin against thee.
—Psalm 119:11

The Bible has been called a "sword of the Spirit"—and that would seem to be an uncomfortable weapon to hide in the heart. But it's a defensive as well as an offensive weapon. It is suitable for protection as well as for attack. The enemy of our souls is Satan. It was he who accosted Jesus in the wilderness, tempting him to forget his mission as the "suffering servant" Messiah and take over Israel as a military and militant Messiah—a plan that was completely contrary to God's salvation plan. Jesus used the sword of the Spirit—the Scriptures—to defeat Satan at his own game, and so may we, if the Word of God is a part of us—hidden in our hearts!

Things to think about:

1. Is "rote memory" what the psalmist is talking about here?
2. If the Scriptures become an integral part of my life, will that make a difference in the way I live?

Because I want the Word to fill my life, I will:

You are the salt of the earth; but if salt has lost its taste, how shall its saltness be restored?

—Matthew 5:13, RSV

Jesus was talking to Christians here—and he was telling his followers that they were the world's preservative, for that was the function of salt in the ancient world. It was used to preserve meat and other perishables. We Christians are all that is holding back the mad rush of the world toward chaos and destruction. It is our righteousness that retards the unrighteousness all around us. Were it not for the presence of a righteous few, God would visit this world in wrath as he once did Sodom and Gomorrah in Abraham's time. As I look at myself, am I fulfilling my task as a preservative? Am I hastening or halting God's kingdom on earth?

Questions to ask myself:
1. Where is the world in God's timetable?
2. Am I making any difference in the lives of people around me?
3. In what ways can I be "salt" in my daily circumstances?

To be "salt" in the world I will:

30 JANUARY

Read 1 Peter 2:11–17

You are the world's light—a city on a hill, glowing in the night for all to see. Don't hide your light! Let it shine for all; let your good deeds glow for all to see, so that they will praise your heavenly Father.
—Matthew 5:14–16, LB

Paul, perhaps the most outstanding follower of Jesus, told the Philippians, "Do all things without grumbling or questioning, that you may be blameless and innocent, children of God without blemish in the midst of a crooked and perverse generation, among whom you shine as lights in the world" (2:14, 15, RSV). Light is a revealer. When a room is in darkness, it could be filled with beauty or ugliness—and no one could tell which. Once the lights are on, however, every corner is revealed. Our function as lights in the world is to reveal the beauty of Jesus wherever we go as naturally as the sun lights the landscape. Since Jesus is *the* Light, all we can do is reflect him! What kind of a reflector am I?

Questions I must confront:
1. What kind of a "light" am I? What is my "power source"?
2. Do people see Jesus in me—or is my light too dim?

To make sure my light is on, I will:

*He said to him the third time, "Simon, son of John, do you love me?"
Peter was grieved because he said to him the third time, "Do you love
me?" And he said to him, "Lord, you know everything; you know that
I love you."*

—John 21:17, RSV

Our personal attachment to Jesus is the primary aspect, and in
the end, the all-important aspect of our own Christian experience.
It is not upon our present achievements or right actions or proper
thinking that our hope for the future rests—but upon our simple
love for Christ and our proper relationship to him. If we cannot
love such a lovable Leader, we lack the basis upon which to build
for the future. But if we truly love him, if our inner being thrills at
his presence, if we look forward eagerly to his Second Coming,
then we know with Paul that "the love of Christ constraineth us" (2
Cor. 5:14). We may have to ask his forgiveness, as Peter doubtless
did, yet the Lover of our souls loves us totally and with complete
acceptance. He seeks only our love in return. Like the Prodigal
Son, we walk into the arms of a loving Father.

For further consideration:
1. Was Peter's love stronger because of his previous denial?
2. Would I be open enough to say "Lord, you know everything; you know that I love you"?

Because of my love for you, Lord, today I will:

1 FEBRUARY

Now those who were scattered went about preaching the word.
—Acts 8:4, RSV

The gospel was intended for the whole world, but our natural tendency as Christians seems to be to clutch it to ourselves. So God had to do something to break us out of our protective shell. His method in the days of the early church, and now, was to allow persecution to come to scatter his children to the four corners of the earth. On their way, they could and can proclaim his message wherever they go. Are we tempted to "hoard" the Word and keep the Good News to ourselves? That's the way the disciples were before the persecution arose, so God had to break them out of their mold and move them out into the world. As the Word goes out, the result will be, "There was much joy in that city" (Acts 8:8, RSV).

Questions to think about and apply:
1. Am I inclined to keep the "Good News" to myself?
2. Where should I be sharing the gospel?
3. How can I best share it?

Today, I will:

For I am not ashamed of the gospel of Christ: for it is the power of God unto salvation to every one that believeth; to the Jew first, and also to the Greek.

—Romans 1:16

How could I be ashamed of this marvelous gospel of Christ? How do I show that shame? Paul, who wrote thus to the Romans, also wrote to his spiritual son, Timothy, "Do not be ashamed then of testifying to our Lord . . . but take your share of suffering for the gospel in the power of God" (2 Tim. 1:8, RSV). I may have to experience persecution to get me outside my own little world with the gospel—and I may have to accept my "share of suffering" for the gospel when I do go out—but isn't that better than being ashamed of it? God, grant me grace to be your person in my world.

Questions to think about:
1. How do I "show my shame" concerning the gospel?
2. What can I do to overcome this problem?
3. I wonder how God feels about it. . . .

Beginning today, I will:

Cast thy burden upon the Lord, and he shall sustain thee: he shall never suffer the righteous to be moved.

—Psalm 55:22

The circumstances of her life she could not alter, but she took them to the Lord, and handed them over into his management; and then she believed that he took it, and she left all the responsibility and the worry and anxiety with him. As often as the anxieties returned she took them back; and the result was that, although the circumstances remained unchanged, her soul was kept in perfect peace in the midst of them. And the secret she found so effectual in her outward affairs, she found to be still more effectual in her inward ones, which were in truth even more utterly unmanageable. She abandoned her whole self to the Lord, with all that she was and all that she had; and, believing that he took that which she had committed to him, she ceased to fret and worry, and her life became all sunshine in the gladness of belonging to Him.

HANNAH WHITALL SMITH (1832–1911)

For further thought:
1. What is the difference between trust in God and anxiety about the future?
2. What significant person in my life best exemplifies this attitude of trust in God?

Because I trust in God, today I will:

And the king's servants said unto the king, Behold, thy servants are ready to do whatsoever my lord the king shall appoint.

—2 Samuel 15:15

If we are really, and always, and equally ready to do whatsoever the King appoints, all the trials and vexations arising from any change in his appointments, great or small, simply do not exist. If he appoints me to work there, shall I lament that I am not to work here? If he appoints me to wait indoors today, am I to be annoyed because I am not to work out-of-doors? If I meant to *write* his messages this morning, shall I grumble because he sends interrupting visitors, rich or poor, to whom I am to *speak* them, or "show kindness" for his sake, or at least obey his command, "Be courteous"? If all my members are really at his disposal, why should I be put out if today's appointment is some simple work for my hands or errands for my feet, instead of some seemingly more important doing of head or tongue?

FRANCES RIDLEY HAVERGAL (1836–1879)

For further thought:
1. Are there some duties in my life that seem more onerous than others?
2. What duties for God do I most enjoy?

In happy service to God, today I will:

I appeal to you, therefore, brethren, by the mercies of God, to present your bodies as a living sacrifice, holy and acceptable to God, which is your spiritual worship.

—Romans 12:1, RSV

Paul could have been a lawyer (perhaps he was!), so carefully does he construct his case for sacrificial living. In the previous chapters of Romans, he has reminded his readers of Christ's sacrifice for them—and now he calls upon them to live a life dedicated to the kingdom of God. Let's face it—it is sometimes easier to die for Christ than to live for him! Yet living is what Paul is calling for. This kind of living involves *daily dying* to self and selfishness. Am I ready for this? God has no place in his program for a selfish servant—he needs *selfless* servants. My worship will work itself out in practical service to others rather than my own selfish pursuits.

Things to think about:
1. What does it mean to be a "sacrifice"?
2. Can a "living sacrifice" hold anything back?
3. What do I think about when I see Christ as a "living sacrifice"?

In view of all this, I will:

The Lord is my light and my salvation; whom shall I fear? The Lord is the strength of my life; of whom shall I be afraid?

—Psalm 27:1

Darkness is the father of fear—and light dispels it. Jesus Christ came as the "light of the world," and in the face of this fact, how can I be fearful? The Revised Standard Version has, "The Lord is the *stronghold* of my life," and that speaks to me of his ability to protect and watch over me. Psalm 62:2 says, "He only is my rock and my salvation, my fortress, I shall not be greatly moved" (RSV). In Christ I have light to dispel my darkness and strength to replace my weakness. What more could I ask? Why am I still fearful and weak in my witness and my walk?

To think about:
1. If I really believed this, how would I live?
2. Can I go beyond the edge of his care and outside the circle of his light?

Because God is my light and my strength, I will:

I know that thou canst do all things, and that no purpose of thine can be thwarted.

—Job 42:2, RSV

God makes no mistakes in placing his people in this world. Whatever my circumstances I may live a Christ-honoring life. True, it is easier to live "above the circumstances" when things are going well for me—and in the midst of others who share my faith. But how much more important it is to live for Christ "above the circumstances" when faced with difficulties and among those unfriendly to my Christian stand. Job came through victoriously in spite of his difficulties, learning in adversity rather than becoming bitter and complaining. May I do the same.

Questions for thought and application:
1. What does it mean to have a repentant spirit as Job had?
2. What should be my attitude toward my circumstances, knowing that God has put me where I am?

As I face the day I will:

Therefore I tell you, do not worry about your life, what you will eat or drink; or about your body, what you will wear....
—Matthew 6:25, NIV

In *The American Mercury* Dr. Charles H. Mayo said, "Worry affects circulation, the heart, the glands, the whole nervous system. I have never known a man who died from overwork, but many who died from doubt." I'm often tempted to think that worry must be the number one enemy of the Christian faith—even though it seems to be such a respectable sin! But it *is* a sin. Bishop Fulton J. Sheen wrote, "All worry is atheism, because it is a want of trust in God." In 1 Peter 5:7 the apostle tells us, "Cast all your anxieties on him, for he cares about you" (RSV). Do I do that?

Questions for thought and application:
1. Why do I worry?
2. Is there a middle ground between trust and worry?
3. Are there other areas of my life that I worry about besides those Jesus mentions in Matthew 6:25?

Beginning today I will:

9 FEBRUARY

Whether therefore ye eat, or drink, or whatsoever ye do, do all to the glory of God.

—1 Corinthians 10:31

Surely the truth must be, that whatsoever in our daily life is lawful and right for us to be engaged in, is in itself a part of our obedience to God; a part, that is, of our very religion. Whensoever we hear people complaining of obstructions and hindrances put by the duties of life in the way of devoting themselves to God, we may be sure they are under some false view or other. They do not look upon their daily work as the task God has set them, and as obedience due to him. We may go farther and say, not only that the duties of life, be they never so toilsome and distracting, are no obstructions to a life of any degree of inward holiness; but that they are even direct means, when rightly used, to promote our sanctification.

H. E. MANNING (1808–1892)

For further thought:
1. Am I involved in anything now that cannot be done "to the glory of God"?
2. Ephesians 6:7 says, "With good will doing service, as to the Lord, and not to men." What does that mean?

In an attitude of true service to God, today I will:

The Lord hath been mindful of us; he will bless us.... that fear the Lord, both small and great.

—Psalm 115:12,13

What a strength and spring of life, what hope and trust, what glad, unresting energy, is in this one thought—to serve him who is "my Lord," ever near me, ever looking on; seeing my intentions before he beholds my failures; knowing my desires before he sees my faults; cheering me to endeavor greater things, and yet accepting the least; inviting my poor service, and yet, above all, content with my poorer love. Let us try to realize this, whatsoever, wheresoever we be. The humblest and the simplest, the weakest and the most encumbered, may love him not less than the busiest and strongest, the most gifted and laborious. If our heart be clear before him; if he be to us our chief and sovereign choice, dear above all, and beyond all desires; then all else matters little. That which concerns us he will perfect in stillness and in power.

H. E. MANNING (1808–1892)

For further thought:
1. What does it mean that the Lord is "mindful" of us?
2. Among the apostles, Peter was first and his brother Andrew seemed to be last on the list. Which accomplished more in God's eyes?

Lord, in serving you today I will:

Whom shall I send, and who will go for us?
—Isaiah 6:8a

This is a question I must face. Because I am a Christian, there is a prior claim on my life. God is calling me, as he was Isaiah, to a specific task. Before he can reveal to me what he wants me to do, he must have my unquestioning obedience. Going for him may entail traveling a great distance—or he might want me to work for him right here at home. I won't begin to know until I answer as Isaiah did, "Here am I; send me." And the Lord replied, "Go, and tell this people. . . ." It may be that I'm to go to a faraway place to "tell" the gospel message—but more than likely I'm to start "telling" it right where I am. Regardless of where it is—I'm to share *him*. And the best way I can do that is to simply tell others what Jesus means to me, how he fills my life and makes it meaningful.

For further contemplation:
1. Am I telling anyone the gospel story?
2. What is the specific gospel task God is calling me to do?
3. Am I open to the Holy Spirit's leading?

Realizing that I must "listen" to God's voice, I will:

FEBRUARY 12

Be ye therefore ready also; for the Son of man cometh at an hour when ye think not.

—Luke 12:40

Am I living every day as if it were the day of Christ's return? Do I live as if I expect him to return *today?* If I live in that attitude of expectancy, will it make any difference in the way I fill my days? Will my activities change—and will my priorities be altered? Does Isaiah's commission from God to "go and tell" give us a clue as to what our priorities should be? Jesus could come back at any moment. When he does, let me be about "my Father's business"! That's the way to be ready!

For further thought:
1. What kinds of activity fill my days now?
2. If I take God's commission to "go and tell" seriously, will I have to change anything about the way I live my life?

In light of Jesus' imminent return, today I will:

13 FEBRUARY

Beloved, let us love one another; for love is of God, and he who loves is born of God and knows God.

—1 John 4:7, RSV

The spirit of Christian love, if allowed to work deeply and thoroughly in all hearts and lives, will prevent disagreement and dissension among Christians. It will lead us to forget ourselves and think of others, not pushing our own interest unduly or demanding first place, but in honor preferring one another. It will make us willing to serve, to minister, even to stoop down to unloose a brother's shoes. It will make us thoughtful, too, in all our acts, in our manners, in our words. It will make us gentle, kindly, patient, teaching us to be all that Christ would be if He were in our place.

J. R. MILLER (1840–1912)

For further thought:
1. Is it possible to love like this in today's world?
2. How can I love those who are not "like me"?

If I pray, "Lord, help me to love others as I would be loved," today I will:

A new commandment I give to you, that you love one another; even as I have loved you, that you also love one another.

                                         —John 13:34, RSV

What a commandment! Divine love is immeasurable, yet Jesus tells me that I am to love as he loved. Can I measure up? Probably not. But does that excuse me? Definitely not! "As I have loved you" is *agape* love, "in spite of" the recipient rather than "because of." It is a gentle love, but a tough love, too. It has to survive rejection and ridicule, meanness and miserliness. There are those around me whose personalities prick and prod me, whose sharp corners sometimes "scratch and dent" me. If all Christians were angelic (and I was too), it would be quite easy to "love one another"—but since they aren't, I will have to work at loving. Lord, let me be patient instead of proud, forgiving instead of spiteful, kind instead of cruel, loving instead of hateful.

For further thought:
1. What is my source of love?
2. What kind of love is it?
3. Whom do I need to love today?

Today I will show my love by:

15 FEBRUARY

Do not forget to entertain strangers, for by so doing some people have entertained angels without knowing it.

—Hebrews 13:2, NIV

"The time is now!" I've seen that motto, and all of a sudden it makes sense spiritually. Sometimes the door of opportunity opens but once—and if we're not ready to move through it, we miss out permanently. "Afterthoughts" aren't always available, so we must *act* now! The time to show interest in or affection to a sufferer is when he is going through the suffering—not later, even the next day, when it's all over and the person is well again—or dead! How often my best and truest thoughts are *after*thoughts—too late to be of any value. O Lord, let them know I care—but put feet on my prayer!

For further thought:
1. Is there a "stranger" in my life to whom I must minister?
2. Is "entertaining" the same as "showing hospitality"?
3. If so, am I as hospitable as I should be?

Today I'm going to:

Little children, let us stop just saying *we love people, let us really love them, and* show it *by our* actions.

—1 John 3:18, LB

If I'm looking for "motivation for mission," this passage of Scripture really tells it like it is! John pulls no punches. Work in Christ's vineyard, money for missions, gifts for the poor, checks written to help a good cause, even ministry to the sick and suffering—none of these please our Lord if our hearts are not in them. When my motivation is love for Christ pouring out of me to others, then my activities will be in obedience to the heavenly mandate. I need to look honestly into my heart to see what spirit prompts my activity. Jesus asks me, "Lovest thou *me?*" as I complete each piece of work. There is no other truer motive for service than this.

For further thought:
1. Am I guilty of the shallow, surface kind of love that *says* rather than *does?*
2. Do I do good works to be seen of men—or to serve God?
3. What spirit motivates me?

Today I will:

17 FEBRUARY

*Live such good lives among the pagans ["unsaved neighbors"—LB]
that, though they accuse you of doing wrong, they may see your good
deeds and glorify God on the day he visits us.*

—1 Peter 2:12, NIV

Wherever I go my shadow falls on someone else, and they are
either better or worse for my presence. Each one of us has, whether
we want to admit it or not, a silent circle of influence—people
among whom we move and upon whose lives we leave our touch. I
cannot live a day without touching *someone* in some way. My influence depends upon who I *am* rather than what I *do*. Beautiful lives
are a blessing to others, while selfish lives leave chaos in their path.
This is not to denigrate the value of doing good deeds and carrying
out good works. But if my life itself is noble, beautiful, Christlike
and holy, a benediction upon those with whom I come in contact,
my good deeds will be multiplied many times over.

For further consideration:
1. Who are some of the people on whom my "shadow" fell
   today?
2. What kind of an influence did I have as I walked my
   world?
3. Am I a benediction or a burden?

I want to be a blessing and be blessed as well, so I will:

Let your light so shine before men, that they may see your good works and give glory to your Father who is in heaven.
—Matthew 5:16, RSV

Every Christian "preaches by influence." There is not a Christian alive who could not preach a sermon every day, at home or out among his neighbors and friends, wherever that might be. It is the beauty of holiness in my common life that will attract others to Christ—not the words of my mouth, however learned they might be. I "preach by shining"—my silent influence should touch other lives with blessing. People should feel stronger, better, happier when they touch a Christian life. Our very faces should shine with goodness and inner glory—not because of who we are, but because of who Christ is in us. How do I measure up to this standard of excellence?

For further thought:
1. When does "silent witness" become a cop-out?
2. Where do I need to shine today?
3. Does my life glorify my heavenly Father?

Today I will "shine" by:

19 FEBRUARY

And the God of all grace, who called you to his eternal glory in Christ, after you have suffered a little while, will himself restore you and make you strong, firm and steadfast.

—1 Peter 5:10, NIV

There are "blessings in tribulation." After I have gone through a season of suffering and can stand beyond it looking back, there should be a new light in my eye, a new glow in my face, a new gentleness in my touch, a new hope in my heart—and a new consecration in my life. I ought not to hang back in the shadows of sorrow; I must move out of them, radiant with the light of victory and peace, willing to step into a place of service and ministry. The comfort that God alone can give puts new joy in my step and gives me a new baptism of love and power.

For further thought:

1. How do I usually react to problems and difficulties?
2. If exercise builds physical muscles, what kind of activities will build spiritual "muscles"?

Today I will:

But by the grace of God I am what I am, and his grace toward me was not in vain. On the contrary, I worked harder than any of them, though it was not I, but the grace of God which is with me.

—1 Corinthians 15:10, RSV

The Christian life is not "pie in the sky"—it's hard work. If loving my fellow Christian takes love from a divine source, think what supernatural love is required of me when I set out to love those who are not of "like precious faith." God's plan for me is "to will and to work for his good pleasure" (Phil. 2:13, RSV). Outside of his will I'll be as useless and ineffective as a tire spinning in snow or mud. But if my life is directed by his will and plan, then I'll say with the apostle Paul, "I worked harder than any of them..." out of the sheer joy of my relationship with him. May my deepest desire be, first of all, to discover his will, and secondly, to carry it out!

For further thought:
1. Am I really ready to make this commitment?
2. What might it involve in terms of "work"?
3. What is my place of service here and now?

As a "worker for God" I will:

21 FEBRUARY

Therefore with joy shall ye draw water out of the wells of salvation.
—Isaiah 12:3

Somehow this passage reminds me of the words of Jesus to the Samaritan woman in John 4:10, "Jesus answered her, 'If you knew the gift of God and who it is that asks you for a drink, you would have asked him and he would have given you living water'" (NIV). The well of my salvation is bottomless and exhaustless. It is deep, its water sweet and eternal. The well of my salvation will never dry up, for it is filled with the "living water" Jesus promised the Samaritan woman. If I experience periods of depression, it's because I am not going to the well for a refill in my life. When my burdens exhaust me and my activities drain me, I need to replenish my life at Jesus' well!

For further thought:
1. Might one of my problems be that I am trying to hold this living water in a leaky bucket?
2. What kind of container should I be using?
3. When is the best time for me to go back to the "well"?
4. How can I do this?

Today I will:

FEBRUARY 22

Let all that you do be done in love.
—1 Corinthians 16:14, RSV

Love must underlie everything I do if I'm to be the kind of Christian God can use. My attitude lies at the heart of my actions. If I do something for someone grudgingly and with a pouting spirit, it would be better for me not to do anything at all. Even Paul says, "Each one must do as he has made up his mind, not reluctantly or under compulsion, for God loves a *cheerful* giver" (2 Cor. 9:7, RSV, italics mine). How do I measure up on God's yardstick? O Lord, help me to give unselfishly of myself to others—including you!

For further thought:
1. If I do a good deed but grumble and complain all the time about the inconvenience it is causing me (or whatever), have I really done the good deed?
2. Is it possible to be considered a Christian "in name only" because of my attitudes?
3. What do I need to do today to change the direction of my life?

To show love today, I will:

... the sheep hear his voice, and he calls his own sheep by name and leads them out.

—John 10:3, RSV

Our heavenly Father has a definite plan for our lives. God does not merely make souls and send them out into this world to take bodies and grow up amid crowds of other souls with bodies, to take their chances and make what they can of their destinies. He plans specifically for each of our lives. He deals with us as individuals. He knows us by name, and loves us each one with a love as distinct and personal as if each was the only child he had on this earth. His plan for each life is always a beautiful plan, too, for he never designs marring and ruin for a life. He never made a human soul for the express purpose of being lost. God's design for each life is that it shall reach a holy character, do a good work in the world, fill a worthy place, however humble, and fill it well, so as to honor God and bless the world.

For further thought:
1. Do I really believe this is true—that God has a plan for me?
2. Am I following God's plan?

Today I will:

Therefore, as God's chosen people, holy and dearly loved, clothe yourselves with compassion, kindness, humility, gentleness and patience.

—Colossians 3:12, NIV

There is a high price to pay for goodness. We can never bless the world by merely having a good time in it. We must suffer, give, and sacrifice, if we would do good to others. Some of us know what self-repression, what self-restraint, what self-crucifixion, and what long, severe discipline lie behind calmness, peacefulness, sweetness of disposition, good temper, kindly feelings, and habitual thoughtfulness.

Most of us have lived long enough to know that these qualities do not come naturally. We have to learn to be good-tempered, thoughtful, gentle, even to be courteous, and the learning is always hard. Indeed we attain nothing good or beautiful in spiritual life without cost. The fruits of the Spirit are promised to and in us— but they come at the cost of *working* them out in our daily lives.

For further thought:

1. If these good fruits in the life come as a result of the Holy Spirit's working, why do *I* have to give of myself?
2. Is goodness attained by "just relaxing" and letting God do it in me?

Today I will:

25 FEBRUARY

Read 1 Corinthians 3:18–23

For the wisdom of this world is foolishness in God's sight.
—1 Corinthians 3:19, NIV

Never before in the history of the world has there been greater emphasis on higher education. In spite of increasing costs for education, our schools in many cases are bulging with students eager to prepare themselves for life. They look to science and philosophy, and the other disciplines, to prepare them for productive and happy lives. Yet Paul says here that all this worldly knowledge is foolishness. What did he mean? We know that Jesus is the Truth as well as the Way and Life. Knowledge not centered in him can be empty and worthless. If I reject him who is the Light of the World, how can I do anything but stumble through the darkness of my own desires, centered in my own reason?

To think about later:
1. If all worthwhile knowledge is centered in Christ, is the world's knowledge worthless for the Christian? Does this mean that Christians should not go to public schools or universities?
2. Where does the world's knowledge ungoverned by allegiance to Christ seem to be sending us?
3. What can I personally do about it?

Today I will:

We are therefore Christ's ambassadors, as though God were making his appeal through us....
—2 Corinthians 5:20, NIV

There is an echo here of God's commission to Isaiah—and his Great Commission through Matthew, "Go and make disciples of all nations..." (Matt. 28:19, NIV). Only the best citizens and statesmen of integrity should be ambassadors, for that task of representing a nation in a foreign land requires the best if it is to be done right. Quality is vitally important in ambassadors—and for Christ's ambassadors it is doubly important that they be "his lights" in a dark land. He is making his "appeal through us...." And that's not an everyday chore. It's the most important task I can perform!

To think about later:
1. Does it make any difference to my responsibility whether or not I have volunteered to be an "ambassador"?
2. In what ways can I be an ambassador—and where do I begin?
3. What does honesty and integrity have to do with it?

Before I can be Christ's ambassador I must:

27 FEBRUARY

Yet you refuse to come to me that you might have life.
— John 5:40, RSV

Life comes in a pretty big package. It doesn't consist simply of getting through with a certain amount of success, a fair amount of creature comforts—enough food to eat, and sufficient clothing to keep ourselves warm. There's much more to life than the mere physical dimension with which we tend to become pretty preoccupied. Real life involves growing into the very image of Christ, into solid spiritual strength and a well-rounded character, into disciplined adulthood—and perhaps most important of all, into the blessed consciousness of the peace of God which he alone can bring. The Peace into which he guides us involves victory over all our trials, even though we must continue to go through them, experiencing a quietness and confidence in our Savior which no outside circumstances can disturb.

For further thought:
1. How much do my circumstances govern my attitude toward life?
2. What characteristics of Jesus reveal his attitude toward his life?
3. Who's in charge of my life?

Because life is such a big package, I'll look to the Lord for:

With my whole heart I seek thee; let me not wander from thy commandments!

—Psalm 119:10, RSV

Christian character isn't born overnight! If we want souls that are strong and noble, beautiful in their reflection of the image of God, we must expect them to grow that way only through our personal search and lengthy pondering. We can't stay in a spiritual kindergarten and expect to graduate magna cum laude! The easy things we learned at the beginning will have to give way to the deeper things of the Spirit as we grow in grace. The things beyond are glorious in their contemplation, but there is a peace and victory available here and now. The Word of God can get into my heart to dwell there and transform me only as I take time to ponder and apply it.

For further thought:
1. What place does the Word of God have in my life right now?
2. How can I make it more prominent and practical?
3. How do I "wander" from it—and what can I do to protect myself from wandering?

Today I will:

Those who know your name will trust in you, for you, Lord, have never forsaken those who seek you.

—Psalm 9:10, NIV

God shows his face to his children when they come to him in prayer. David's whole life made that clear, and in this psalm in particular I get the impression that David was preeminently a man of prayer. Only in prayer can we discover how glorious God is—and how vulnerable and approachable he is. As I spend time with him in prayer, the sweet gifts of his love come down upon me and I am transformed into his likeness.

The busier my day, the more prayer I need. In the quiet moments with you, O God, I gain the serenity to face my hectic, feverish day. My prayer brings a little heaven to my soul and makes me stronger for service.

For further contemplation:
1. David never neglected to give God thanks, even when he was crying out for help. Is my prayer life thankful—or fretful?
2. Am I perhaps too busy with the mundane to pray about the important?

As I come to God in prayer today, I will:

MARCH 2

She said to herself, "If I only touch his cloak, I will be healed."
—Matthew 9:21, NIV

This woman's need and her sorrow stirred Jesus' heart. Time and again during his ministry Jesus took time out to sympathize with those who hurt, to lift up those who struggled and who knew grief. His heart responded to human need. Every cry of distress struck a responsive chord in his heart. His heart is still the same. I need to remember that. When I reach out my weary hand, and my fearful fingertip of faith touches the hem of his garment, he turns to tell me, "Take heart... your faith has healed you."

For further thought:

1. Is my prayer life as childlike as this woman's... or do I pray more for the benefit of others than for my own needs?
2. What picture do I have in mind when I pray—perhaps Jesus as a divine Superman, or as a heavenly healer? Are images such as these harmful or helpful?

As I pray to God today, I will:

3 MARCH

That is why we never give up. Though our bodies are dying, our inner strength in the Lord is growing every day.
—2 Corinthians 4:16, LB

All lasting blessing comes through the medium of a cross. Nothing builds me better in character than the day-by-day drudgery that makes up so much of life. As I undergo these things, I pray for release from dull routine, duties, rules, the everyday round of the seeming treadmill of life. Yet this is God's school for me—the place where I learn the meaning of my existence. I cannot grow in the midst of an easy way. I must accept the treadmill as it is—the plodding, the routine, even the dullness—and resolve to do my best in the midst of it all. It is only in doing so that I will develop the strong and noble character which is God's plan for me.

For further thought:

1. Do I have a "cross" in my life? If so, how am I handling it?
2. Is the "discipline of drudgery" a part of God's plan for me?

As I face my world today, I will:

You shall eat in plenty and be satisfied, and praise the name of the Lord your God, who has dealt wondrously with you.

—Joel 2:26, RSV

These words sum up for me God's way of giving. He doesn't hand out his bounty in little dribs and drabs. He *pours* out his blessings until we have no more room to receive. He fills my emptiness until my capacity to receive is at its limit. In fact, nothing except my limited ability to take from God limits the supply I get from him. He could keep on giving infinitely, if it were not for my finite capacity to accept. It's too bad we can't be like the little girl who had her own special translation of Psalm 23:1: "The Lord is my shepherd, that's all I want." The sole reason we don't have more of God's riches is the smallness of our faith—that's the only obstacle that stands in the way of our being fully blest.

For further thought:
1. Do I really believe God has "dealt wondrously with me"?
2. Do I have any hidden grudges against God?
3. In what ways do I hinder the full working of his Spirit within me?

Today I will "let go and let God" fill me to the fullest by:

5 MARCH

Keep your life free from love of money, and be content with what you have; for he [God] has said, "I will never fail you nor forsake you."
—Hebrews 13:5, RSV

These words are reminiscent of Paul's words to Timothy: "But if we have food and clothing, with these we shall be content (satisfied)" (1 Tim. 6:8, AB). Thomas Fuller (1608–1661) must have had these passages in mind when he wrote: "An ounce of contentment is worth a pound of sadness, to serve God with." Another insightful commentator, James Scott, said, "No man is so sad as he who has much and wants more." In our inflationary, hectic society, it seems that we never get enough of material things. We are always demanding more. But perhaps austerity is just around the corner for us, and I'm not too sure but what we'll be closer to God's best plan for us as a result. Lord, help me be content with what I have. Let me live thankfully rather than crankfully.

For further thought:

1. Do I live as if the promise in Hebrews 13:5 were in the Bible?
2. How am I serving God—from a thankful heart or resentfully?
3. Is "contentment" ever wrong?

Today, in view of this scriptural admonition to contentment, I will:

I press on toward the goal to win the prize for which God has called me heavenward in Christ Jesus.

—Philippians 3:14, NIV

It wasn't only the old stalwarts of the faith like Paul who had deep spiritual insight. A young man of only twenty-two—Jim Elliot—once wrote, "He is no fool who gives what he cannot keep to gain what he cannot lose." Only a few short years later Elliott died a martyr's death at the hands of the Auca Indians on a sandy riverbank in Ecuador. At an early age this young man had learned the same lesson as the apostle Paul—our goal in life needs to have eternity's values in view. We need to have the heavenly vision if we are to keep our earthly life in proper perspective. Lord, let me seek the proper prize, the one that will last throughout eternity.

For further thought:
1. What is the most important thing to me right now?
2. Where are my priorities—and do I need to change the direction of my life?

Today I will seek to:

... whoever wants to become great among you must be your servant, and whoever wants to be first must be slave of all.

—Mark 10:43, 44, NIV

Humility is the grace that shines most brightly in the Christian's arsenal of availability to God. Whenever my own selfish interests come into play, they mar the beauty of what I am doing for God and my fellowmen. I must try to do my work quietly, not drawing attention to myself to let others know I'm involved. If I am content to pour my life into others without thought of recompense, letting Christ have all the honor, then I will be fulfilling the command Jesus gave here. I must work for God's eyes only, seeking to be a blessing rather than to gain a blessing for myself.

For further thought:
1. Will this "others first" philosophy work in the marketplace?
2. Are "humility" and "love" synonymous?
3. Is "What would Jesus do?" a workable question today?

As a "servant" today I will:

... Let steadfastness have its full effect, that you may be perfect and complete, lacking in nothing.

—James 1:4, RSV

It's easy to grow discouraged regarding spiritual progress. Year after year it seems that I struggle with my bad temper or ugly disposition, my selfishness and pride—and I don't seem to be winning the battle. But my Savior is a patient teacher who never loses his temper because of my slowness to learn or my failure to understand. Over and over he teaches me the same lesson until finally I learn it. Spiritual maturity is not gained overnight—nor will it pass away like a whiff of smoke once it *is* learned. How thankful I am that my patient heavenly Father is in the training business. May I be teachable!

For further consideration:

1. What does it mean to be "perfect and complete"?
2. If God be for me, who can be against me?
3. Is there any way I can learn to show God's patience to the "significant others" in my life?

To "let steadfastness have its full effect" in me today, I will:

9 MARCH

When Moses went and told the people all the Lord's words and laws, they responded with one voice, "Everything the Lord has said we will do."

—Exodus 24:3, NIV

Decision time *must* come. As Elijah told the Israelites of his day, we cannot keep on wavering "between two opinions." ("If the Lord is God, follow him; but if Baal is God, follow him"—1 Kings 18:21, NIV.) I simply cannot go on vacillating from opinion to opinion, never taking a definite stand. When the Israelites decided to *obey*, they also decided to *act*: "Everything the Lord has said we will *do*!" With decision to obey comes responsibility to "do," to follow.

In Matthew 12:30 Jesus said, "He who is not with me is against me." There is no neutral ground or gray area, no place for indecision and procrastination. Deciding not to decide is a decision in itself. Christ stands before me today and demands a decision. A decision to "hedge" is a decision against Jesus.

For further thought:
1. Am I guilty of "wavering"?
2. In what way am I wavering right now?
3. What will I do about it?

Today God is telling me to:

... I have learned to be content whatever the circumstances.
—Philippians 4:11, NIV

It is necessary to distinguish between contentment and satisfaction. I am to strive to be content in any situation or set of circumstances, but I am never to be "satisfied" in this world regardless of circumstances, whether they be prosperous or difficult. *Satisfaction* will come only when I reach heaven's glory to spend eternity with him. I am not to seek *contentment* by repressing my soul's desires. Yet I am as a Christian to live in the midst of my circumstances calmly and peacefully, resting my soul's desires in him—wholly independent of the turmoil around me, and undisturbed by that which would disquiet me. Content in whatever situation, yet never self-satisfied—that's what it means to be a Christian.

For further thought:
1. Am I in danger of being "self-satisfied"?
2. How am I handling what life dishes out to me right now?

Today I will:

11 MARCH

If you ask anything in my name, I will do it.

—John 14:14, RSV

God not only has a better way of giving (see Joel 2:26), but he also has a better answer for my prayers than I could ever dream of. Many times he answers my prayers by lifting me to himself, rather than by bringing his will down to mine. Thus I grow stronger, so that I need not go to him with the petty little things that bother me. Now I can bear the heavier burden without begging him to lighten it. And the sorrow that would once have buried me can now be borne, because I have grown up in God. Peace can come in the midst of trial because I walk daily with the Prince of Peace himself. I don't need to be delivered from the battle, for he is with me *in* it. Victory in the conflict is better than freedom from conflict.

For further thought:
1. As I think upon the vitality of Jesus' prayer life, what seems to be missing from mine?
2. What is involved in asking or praying in "Jesus' name"?

As I pray today, I will:

Why do [I] seek the speck that is in [my] brother's eye, but do not notice the log that is in [my] own eye?

—Matthew 7:3, RSV

A good caption for this verse would be "looking for logs"! I seem to be so prone to discover my neighbor's *little* faults (specks) and completely overlook my own log-sized blemishes. Somehow, along with the rest of the human race, I have a keener eye for the flaws of others than for their loveliness. How often do I gossip about the good points of my neighbors? Don't I usually play up their faults and forget their strong points? If only I could change this propensity to "look for specks" and begin to see my own "logs" against the backdrop of my neighbor's strengths instead of his weaknesses.

For further consideration:
1. In what ways and with whom do I "look for logs"?
2. How can I overcome this propensity?
3. What are my own "logs"?

Today I will begin looking upon others through Jesus' eyes and:

13 MARCH

Surely God is my salvation; I will trust and not be afraid. The Lord, the Lord, is my strength and my song; he has become my salvation.
—Isaiah 12:2, NIV

It will not save me to know that Christ is a Savior; but it will save me to trust him to be my Savior. I shall not be delivered from the wrath to come by believing that his atonement is sufficient; but I shall be saved by making that atonement my trust, my refuge, and my all. The pith, the essence of faith lies in this—a casting of oneself on the promise. It is not the life jacket on board ship that saves the man when he is drowning, nor is it his belief that it is an excellent and successful invention. No! He must have it around him, or he will sink.

C. H. SPURGEON (1834–1892)

For further thought:
1. What does it mean to know personally that God is my salvation?
2. What part does trust or commitment play in this matter of salvation?

In the light of my salvation, today I will:

Do you not know that in a race all the runners compete, but only one receives the prize? So run that you may obtain it.
　　　　　　　　　　　　　　　　　—1 Corinthians 9:24, RSV

Concentration is the key to success in any area of life. This is strikingly true in sports—running in particular. The ability to center one's attention on the course ahead and shut out distractions often wins the race. In the spiritual realm, concentration is just as important. One of Satan's frequent ploys is to distract the believer. If he sees a Christian concentrating on the important matters, he moves in to distract that individual and trick him into aiming his energies at a different goal. With Paul, we must say, "... *this one thing* I do, forgetting those things which are behind, and reaching forth unto those things which are before" (Phil. 3:13, italics mine).

For further thought:
1. What are my immediate spiritual goals?
2. What are my long-range goals?
3. What's the *first step* I must take to reach them?

Today I will take that first step and:

15 MARCH

Give me understanding, and I will keep your law and obey it with all my heart.

—Psalm 119:34, NIV

One wonders if Solomon was aware of this psalm when he prayed for wisdom (1 Kings 3:3–14) to be a good king and a worthy successor of his father David. Here in Psalm 119 the psalmist is praying for enlightenment and understanding, for the necessary wisdom to love consistently. I must pray such a prayer every day of my life. I will never reach the point of independence from God. In verse 35 the psalmist goes on to ask for a "directed" inclination. He asks the Lord to "turn" his heart toward righteousness—he even asks God to literally force him into righteous acts. "Teach me" to follow the commandments of God, he prays in verse 33. My prayers should include all these aspects of asking, that I might exhibit the fruit of the Spirit in my Christian walk. The question is, Do I?

For further consideration:

1. Have I ever sincerely prayed this prayer for guidance?
2. Is there a specific need in my life right now that I could lift up to God?

Today I will pray:

So Jesus grew both tall and wise, and was loved by God and man.
—Luke 2:52, LB

If I want to bring glory to my heavenly Father I must grow spiritually. To grow, I must have a willingness to learn and to gain understanding. When Hannah prayed, God sent her Samuel. But along with the joy of a son, God sent her and Elkanah the spiritual perception to surrender that son to the service of God (1 Sam. 1 and 2). When King Solomon asked for wisdom that he might rightly rule Israel, God answered him abundantly. And God will honor my sincere prayer if I desire spiritual growth and maturity to use in his service. Just as in the physical realm "we are what we eat," so our spiritual growth is governed by our spiritual diet. What am I eating spiritually?

For further thought:
1. Are there any signs of growth in my life?
2. Are there specific areas where I need to grow?

To help myself grow today, I will:

Lo, I am with you always, to the close of the age.
> —Matthew 28:20, RSV

The Modern Language Bible has "all the days" in place of "always" in this scripture. That's even more emphatic. It's a comfort to learn that the Lord prepares a blessing for each day, coming to us every morning to offer it to us personally, making himself available to walk with us through our daily situation. Too often my days are dull or routine, and I wonder if he is really interested in me. The fact that I do not recognize his presence does not mean he has left me—it simply means that my spiritual eyes are momentarily blinded by the world around me. If I will but realize this, my walk will be such that, wherever I go, he will be my Companion and Comforter.

For further thought:
1. What changes do I need to make in my life since he is with me "always"?
2. What about my attitudes toward the things that happen to me daily?

Since he is with me "all the days," I will:

Yet I will rejoice in the Lord, I will joy in the God of my salvation.
—Habakkuk 3:18, RSV

As the psalmist makes clear, the "joy of salvation" comes from contact and communion with God. Prayer is the vehicle of that contact and communication. Without prayer, Christian joy is unattainable, for joy can only be nurtured and sustained by prayer. It is scripturally valid to say that a prayerless Christian is a joyless Christian, and a joyless Christian is a powerless Christian.

Many years ago, a tailor's shop had been burned in the great Chicago fire. The next morning the tailor walked to the ruins carrying a table. Setting it up in the charred debris, he raised over it this sign: "Everything lost except wife, children, and hope. Business will be resumed as usual tomorrow morning." The Christian's joy is just as resilient. It doesn't depend on circumstances. Rather it towers above circumstances because its source is *in God.* My communion with him taps exhaustless resources.

For further thought:
1. Where do I expect to find my joy?
2. Am I to rejoice because of or in spite of my circumstances?
3. What are some circumstances under which I find it particularly difficult to be joyful?

Lord, help me look to you as my Source of joy. Today let me:

Another of the disciples said to him, "Lord, let me first go and bury my father."

—Matthew 8:21, RSV

Two short words unveil this man's attitude toward Christ: "Me first." Usually our words, sooner or later, do reveal the attitude of our hearts. Unfortunately I, too, sometimes say "me first" by my attitudes—not only toward Jesus but toward my fellow Christians as well. In this case, the man was using his father as an excuse for not following Jesus. Is there anything wrong with putting parents first in our lives—honoring them, as the Bible tells us to do? The noteworthy thing here was that the man's father was not yet dead! This phrase was simply a figure of speech designed to sound sanctimonious and to give the impression that the man really wanted to fulfill his filial responsibility. So many of our excuses are like this— fabrications rather than facts. Lord, I want to be a true disciple, wholeheartedly surrendered to your will. Help me not to say *"me first"*!

For further thought:
1. What are some of my excuses for not following Jesus daily?
2. What are some of the duties I rank higher than I do my Savior?

Putting Christ first, today I will:

Put off your old nature ... and be renewed in the spirit of your minds, and put on the new nature, created after the likeness of God....

—Ephesians 4:22–24, RSV

I cannot possibly live the Christian life on my own power. It's so encouraging to note that Paul says I have a new nature "created" for me! God doesn't expect me to live the Christian life in my own strength. Rather, as Paul says in Ephesians 2:10 (RSV), "We are his workmanship...." We possess an entirely new source of life—the Lord Jesus himself. He overcame the obstacles in his way by supernatural power, and we can do the same. I can live the overcoming life because I'm connected to the Overcomer. My only responsibility is to accept what he has provided and move ahead in that strength. By so doing, I can move into "... true righteousness and holiness" (v.24) as he desires. It's great to know that obedience is mine—he provides the means.

For further thought:
1. What are my specific problems with the old nature?
2. Is "putting off" my old nature possible?

Today I will deal with this specific problem:

Happy is he whose help is the God of Jacob, whose hope is in the Lord his God.

—Psalm 146:5, RSV

Most translations of this passage use the word "blessed" here. Unfortunately, "happy" has been so overused as to suffer almost the same fate as "love." It has been watered down for popular use so that it can mean everything from "apt" to "lucky." Lasting contentment or deep joy is probably closest to the psalmist's meaning here. Happiness is an elusive thing. To grab for it is to destroy it. O. G. Wilson once wrote: "Happy is the soul that has something to look backward to with pride, and something to look forward to with hope." True happiness comes only to those whose God is the Lord, those who find their "hope" in him. Another writer has said: "We are no longer happy as soon as we wish to be happier." Happiness is not gained by trying. Rather, it is learned—it grows out of experiencing complete surrender to God, a yielding without reserve.

For further thought:
1. Do I live in the light of this verse?
2. Did Jesus live in its light?

Lord, let me lean back into your love today and show my happiness by:

He said, "Throw your net on the right side of the boat and you will find some." When they did, they were unable to haul the net in because of the large number of fish.

—John 21:6, NIV

There is a striking lesson here. Briefly put, decision decides destiny. When the disciples did as Jesus told them, deciding to obey his command, they accomplished what they could not do alone. Before, they had caught no fish because they were fishing without Jesus. As they chose to obey him, they were successful in that which they had set out to do; they had more fish than they could handle! As we step out in faith to follow Jesus' command, whatever it might be, we will be surprised to see a path open up before us where there was nothing but obstacles before. The key is in stepping out at Jesus' command. Obedience means to move out into God's plan for me a step at a time.

For further thought:
1. What specific step is Jesus telling me to take today?
2. What commands of his have I refused to follow? Which have I obeyed?
3. What kind of "fishing" does he want me to do?

In obedience to Jesus' command, today I will:

23 MARCH

When Jesus saw their faith, he said to the paralytic, "Son, your sins are forgiven."

—Mark 2:5, NIV

Faith has already been mentioned several times in this book—and this account of faith in Jesus on the part of several "pal"-bearers is a classic. The heart of Jesus must have been warmed as he saw the sensitive trust of the men who bore their paralyzed friend into his presence. This story of faith reveals an often-overlooked aspect of true faith—its basic unselfishness. My faith should not only be large—it should also be other-centered. I should not allow selfish personal concerns to obliterate my concern for others. I should be so gripped by concern for others that I will give myself unselfishly and unstingingly to others. As I actively reach out in concern to others, my own anxieties and concerns will fade into the background. That's what happened to the men in our text—and it can happen to me!

For further thought:
1. How could I describe my faith?
2. Do I reach out and touch others with my faith—or is it self-centered?

Lord, today I'll let my faith show by:

By the blessing of the upright a city is exalted, but it is overthrown by the mouth of the wicked.

—Proverbs 11:11, RSV

I can apply every word of this passage to myself. It is my deepest desire to be one of the "righteous" the writer refers to here. I'm not talking about *self*-righteousness, but the righteousness only God can impart. I want the blanket of God's righteousness over me. As his righteousness blankets my being, I can then move out into my world and be a "blessing" as the text suggests. Some anonymous wise man has said, "A year of self-surrender will bring larger blessings than fourscore years of selfishness." I want to surrender myself in service to others—not for my own gain, but for theirs.

For further thought:

1. Am I being honest with myself and God when I say the words of the last sentence?
2. Is there some service I can render to someone right now?

Lord, help me today to:

25 MARCH

You shall be careful to do therefore as the Lord your God has commanded you; you shall not turn aside to the right hand or to the left.
—Deuteronomy 5:32, RSV

God is a kind Father. He sets us all in the places where he wishes us to be employed; and that employment is truly "our Father's business." He chooses work for every creature which will be delightful to them, if they do it simply and humbly. He gives us always strength enough, and sense enough, for what he wants us to do.

F. B. MEYER (1847–1929)

For further thought:
1. Am I doing those things God would have me to do, and does what I am doing glorify him?
2. Do I have a goal in my spiritual life, a place I want to reach, a task I want supremely to accomplish for him?

In pursuit of my spiritual goal, today I will:

Do you not know that you are God's temple and God's Spirit dwells in you?

—1 Corinthians 3:16, RSV

We read in a British publication about a young German doctor, now an earnest Christian but once a member of Hitler Youth and a soldier in Hitler's army. Speaking in a British church, he said: "I am concerned with the casual quality of the faith of youth. You do not give to Christ anything like the devotion which German youth once gave to Hitler."

"God hath said, I will dwell in them and walk in them; and I will be their God, and they shall be my people." Such dignity and honor conferred upon us cause the soul to bow low in humiliation at the foot of the cross. If we are the temple of the living God, we must be holy. We must submit our will to God's will. We must strive to live daily as pleases him and as becomes holiness.

OLIVER G. WILSON

For further thought:
1. How much of my devotion am I truly giving God?
2. What in my life right now must I give up if I am to be a fit temple for God's Spirit to indwell?

As I look at my life through this lens of Scripture, today I will:

Catch us... the little foxes, that spoil the vineyards, for our vineyards are in blossom.

—Song of Solomon 2:15, RSV

We talk about little sins, but when we remember that every sin is committed against the infinite God, and that all sins are eternal in their influences and consequences, the smallest sin grows to tremendous importance. Indeed, there are no small matters in moral life. How do we know what is small or what is great in God's eye or as measured by its results through future ages? True faithfulness is not careless in little things. It is harder always to be faithful in small, obscure, unpraised things than in things that are brilliant and conspicuous. More persons fail in doing the little things, the common prosaic things, of everyday life than in doing the greater and more prominent things. Hence it is here that we need to keep double watch upon ourselves. All fraying out of character begins with one little thread left loose.

J. R. MILLER (1840–1912)

For further thought:
1. What "little foxes" trouble my vineyard?
2. Do I have one problem more prominent than any other?

Today I will watch out for:

And he said unto them, Take heed, and beware of covetousness: for a man's life consisteth not in the abundance of the things which he possesseth.

—Luke 12:15

There is such a thing as spiritual poverty. We are greedy after the things of this world, and can never get enough of them; but of the real things, the things that will last through eternity, we seem to be satisfied with very small portions. "What seek ye?" asks the Master, his hands filled with precious blessings; and we ask for some little things, some trifle, when we might have glorious fulness of blessing. How very strange it must seem to the angels to see us poor mortals giving our lives, our very souls, to secure some temporal thing of earth that will perish tomorrow, and then not taking the precious spiritual blessings that we might have for the mere asking!

For further thought:
1. What is most important to me right now?
2. What do I want more than anything else at this time in my life?

Today I will:

*Then he said to the man, "Stretch out your hand." And the man
stretched it out, and it was restored, whole like the other.*
—Matthew 12:13, RSV

What a striking illustration this is of what it means to be "saved
by grace"! In the midst of the Pharisees' plot to entrap him, Jesus
took time out to heal this man with the deformed hand. What the
man could not do for himself, Jesus did for him. His only responsibility was to "stretch out your hand." In this process called salvation, our responsibility is to "stretch out" and grasp the hand God
has already extended to us. Only he can meet our need—and there
is no way we can "earn" or merit his help. All we can do is accept.
The verb used here—*restore*—beautifully pictures the process. Our
original relationship to God our Creator was severed by Adam's act
of disobedience in the Garden. Fellowship with God was thus broken, and it is only when we as individuals come back to God in
humility and repentance, admitting our sin and our emptiness, that
he can "restore" that broken relationship. Lord, help me to turn
over my sick self to you as this man did!

For further thought:
1. Is this episode descriptive of my own conversion
   experience?
2. In what ways do I "break fellowship" with God by disobedience even now?

Today I will:

And to the centurion Jesus said, "Go; be it done for you as you have believed." And the servant was healed at that very moment.
                                                    —Matthew 8:13, RSV

Here's another example of restoration—and this whole episode illustrates an additional aspect of salvation, the place of faith in the whole process. Is it possible that the smallness of our faith limits God? What if this Roman centurion hadn't had great faith in Christ's ability to heal his servant? This is a provocative, mysterious question that probably won't be answered this side of eternity. In a sense, however, this question *has* been answered—in the lives of that host of bold Christians who have been the activists in the church since it began centuries ago. The formula seems to be: small faith—small accomplishments, large faith—large accomplishments. Those who *dare* much spiritually seem to be those who accomplish much in that realm. Those who fear launching out in faith never leave the shore! Lord, help me to dare to believe you for miracles as this centurion did!

For further thought:
1. Has my faith shown signs of "daring" lately?
2. What specifically should I dare to believe today?

In faith today I will:

You call forth songs of joy. You care for the land and water it; you enrich it abundantly... you crown the year with your bounty, and your carts overflow with abundance.

—Psalm 65:8–11, NIV

What a description this is of what the Christian life could and should be! We do God a disservice when we engulf him in "reverent gloom" and bottle him up in "artificial solemnity." Our God is not an austere, forbidding Master. He is the One who caused the psalmist to write that the valleys "shout for joy and sing" (65:13, NIV)! The psalmist also writes of God that he brought his people "to a place of abundance" (66:12, NIV). That doesn't sound like the narrow, sometimes confining ways in which we worship him, does it? The essence of worship is to bring God into *all* our lives—and that is to be abundantly true of all our human moods. Our childlike joys should be the place where we abundantly meet him!

For further thought:
1. Is God a part—is he the *center*—of my life?
2. If not, what areas do I close off to him?

Lord, open my life to all that you have for me. Today I will:

In all your ways acknowledge him, and he will make straight your paths.

—Proverbs 3:6, RSV

The Shepherd knows what pastures are best for his sheep, and they must not question nor doubt, but trustingly follow him. Perhaps he sees that the best pastures for some of us are to be found in the midst of opposition or of earthly trials. If he leads you there, you may be sure they are green for you, and you will grow and be made strong by feeding there. Perhaps he sees that the best waters for you to walk beside will be raging waves of trouble and sorrow. If this should be the case, he will make them still waters for you, and you must go and lie down beside them, and let them have all their blessed influences upon you.

HANNAH WHITALL SMITH (1832–1911)

For further thought:
1. What kind of "waters" am I walking beside?
2. What does it mean to have "straight" paths?

As my Shepherd leads me, today I will:

2 APRIL

Fear of man will prove to be a snare, but whoever trusts in the Lord is kept safe.

—Proverbs 29:25, NIV

God has brought us into this time; he, and not ourselves or some dark demon. If we are not fit to cope with that which he has prepared for us, we should have been utterly unfit for any condition that we imagine for ourselves. In this time we are to live and wrestle, and in no other. Let us humbly, tremblingly, manfully look at it, and we shall not wish that the sun could go back its ten degrees, or that we could go back with it. If easy times are departed, it is that the difficult times may make us more in earnest; that they may teach us not to depend upon ourselves. If easy belief is impossible, it is that we may learn what belief is, and in whom it is to be placed.

F. D MAURICE (1805–1872)

For further thought:

1. What does it mean to be "safe" in the care of the Lord?
2. What does it *really* mean to "trust" in the Lord?

With the Lord as my Guide, today I will:

Let us not therefore judge one another any more: but judge this rather, that no man put a stumblingblock or an occasion to stumble (fall) in his brother's way.

—Romans 14:13

A vexation arises, and our expressions of impatience hinder others from taking it patiently. Disappointment, ailment, or even weather depresses us; and our look or tone of depression hinders others from maintaining a cheerful and thankful spirit. We say an unkind thing, and another is hindered in learning the holy lesson of charity that thinks no evil. We say a provoking thing, and our sister or brother is hindered in that day's effort to be meek. How sadly, too, we may hinder without word or act! For wrong feeling is more infectious than wrong doing; especially the various phases of ill temper,—gloominess, touchiness, discontent, irritability,—do we not know how catching these are?

FRANCES RIDLEY HAVERGAL (1836–1879)

For further thought:
1. Am I guilty of being judgmental?
2. Is there something in my attitude toward others that is a "stumbling block" to them?

As I look at my life, today I will:

4 APRIL

My brethren, count it all joy when ye fall into divers temptations; knowing this, that the trying of your faith worketh patience.

—James 1:2, 3

We have need of patience with ourselves and with others; with those below, and those above us, and with our own equals; with those who love us and those who love us not; for the greatest things and for the least; against sudden inroads of trouble, and under daily burdens; disappointments as to the weather, or the breaking of the heart; in the weariness of the body, or the wearing of the soul; in our own failure of duty, or others' failure toward us; in everyday wants, or in the aching of sickness or the decay of old age; in disappointment, bereavement, losses, injuries, reproaches; in heaviness of the heart; or its sickness amid delayed hopes. In all these things, from childhood's little troubles to the martyr's sufferings, patience is the grace of God, whereby we endure evil for the love of God.

E. B. PUSEY (1800–1832)

For further thought:
1. What recent experiences in my life have taught me patience?
2. What people in my life "try" my patience?
3. How can I put these lessons in patience into practice?

Thank you, Lord, for the lessons I'm learning. Today I will:

In peace I will both lie down and sleep; for thou alone, O Lord, makest me dwell in safety.

—Psalm 4:8, RSV

The number-one enemy of the Christian life seems to be worry and anxiety—fretting about tomorrow. David speaks to this tendency when he prays, "I will lie down in peace and sleep, for though I am alone, O Lord, you will keep me safe" (L.B). Francois de la Mothe Fenelon, French churchman (1651–1715), said: "We sleep in peace in the arms of God when we yield ourselves up to His providence, in a delightful consciousness of His tender mercies; no more restless uncertainties, no more anxious desires, no more impatience at the place we are in; for it is God who has put us there and who holds us in His arms. Can we be unsafe where he has placed us?" Is that the way I feel and live?

For further thought:
1. What is my number-one problem as a Christian?
2. How does this promise from the Psalms apply to that situation?

Today I will:

6 APRIL

Oh, how I love thy law! It is my meditation all the day.
—Psalm 119:97, RSV

I wonder if I can honestly pray this prayer. F. B. Meyer (1847–1929) pointed out: "The Bible seldom speaks, and certainly never its deepest, sweetest words, to those who always read it in a hurry. Nature can only tell her secrets to such as will sit still in her sacred temple till their eyes lose the glare of earthly glory, and their ears are attuned to her voice. And shall revelation do what nature cannot? Never. The man who shall win the blessedness of hearing her must watch daily at her gates and wait at the posts of her doors. There is no chance for a lad to grow, who only gets an occasional mouthful of food and always swallows that in a hurry." Is that the way I eat spiritually? What kind of a spiritual diet do I have?

For further thought:
1. If I really *loved* the Word, how would I treat it differently than I do now?
2. What does it mean in today's terminology to "meditate" daily?

With the Word as my guide today, I will:

And they devoted themselves to the apostles' teaching and fellowship, to the breaking of bread and the prayers.

—Acts 2:42, rsv

J. H. Jowett (1864–1923), the great English preacher who once pastored the prestigious Fifth Avenue Presbyterian Church in New York City, wrote of this text: "This is a concise summary of a Christian life. We must not waste time looking for a creed, but accept some things as settled once and for all; we must seek fellowship for what we can give and get; we must attend scrupulously to our spiritual meals; and by these means shall make ourselves strong for intercessory prayer." As a result of their concentration on the primary things of the faith, these early Christians saw real health evidenced in their church: "And the Lord added to the church daily such as should be saved" (v. 47). What's happening in my church?

For further thought:
1. Does this passage describe my church? Does it summarize my life?
2. Am I really putting first things first in my life? Am I concerned for the things that concern my Lord?

To get my priorities straight, today I will:

The eternal God is your dwelling place, and underneath are the everlasting arms.

—Deuteronomy 33:27, RSV

What a striking and sweeping promise this is to me as a groping Christian. It reminds me of Psalm 90:1, 2: "Lord, thou hast been our dwelling place in all generations. Before the mountains were brought forth, or ever thou hadst formed the earth and the world, even from everlasting to everlasting, thou art God." Am I living my life as if these promises were there for me?

Northcote Deck has written: "One of the original owners of Mount Morgan, in Queensland, who toiled for years on its barren slopes, eking out a miserable living, never knew that underfoot was one of the richest mountains of gold the world has known. Here was wealth, vast, unimagined, yet unrealized, unappropriated. Just so, every believer has, in the wealth of God's promises, a spiritual Mount Morgan under his feet only waiting to be recognized, claimed, and appropriated."

For further thought:
1. What have I missed because of my blindness?
2. What "riches" should I appropriate today?

Today I will:

Whatever your task, work heartily, as serving the Lord and not men.
—Colossians 3:23, RSV

Every common walk of life is glorious with God's presence, if we could but see the glory. We are always under commission from Christ. Every morning we have sealed orders from him. These are opened as the day's events come. Every opportunity for duty or for heroism is a divine call. I must be loyal to duty, no matter where I may hear its call nor to what service it may bid me. Duty is duty, however humble it may be; and divine duty is always noble, because it is what God himself requires. The work which the day brings to us is always his will, and the sweetest thing in all this world to a loving, loyal heart always is God's will. The service of angels in heaven's brightness is no more radiant than the faithful duty-doing of the lowliest saint on earth.

For further thought:
1. What will I be doing today which is a duty given me by God?
2. Can I detect the divine in my daily task?

Since my daily duty is given me by God, today I will:

"If you cling to your life, you will lose it; but if you give it up to me, you will save it."

—Matthew 10:39, LB

The way to make nothing of one's life is to be very careful of it, to hold it back from dangerous duty, from costly service, to save it from the waste of self-denial and sacrifice. The way to make one's life an eternal success is to do with it as Jesus did with his—present it a living sacrifice to God, to be used wholly for him. Men said he threw his life away, and so it certainly seemed up to the morning of his resurrection. But no one would say that now of Christ. His was the throwing away of life which led to its glorifying. In no other way can we make anything worthy and eternal of our life. Saving is losing. It is losing it in devotion to Christ and his service that saves a life for heavenly honor and glory.

For further thought:
1. Am I being "too careful" of my life?
2. What are some ways I am called upon to be a "living sacrifice" in my work situation? At home?
3. Have I ever been called upon to do something downright dangerous because of my Christian commitment?

Today I will:

But the wise took oil in their vessels with their lamps.
—Matthew 25:4

It is important to be prepared. There is a vast difference between worrying about a possible future trial and being ready for it if it should come. The former we should never do; the latter we should always seek to do. The one who is always in shape for physical emergencies—for the hard pinches, the steep climbing, the sharp struggle—gets through life victoriously. In moral and spiritual matters the principle is the same. Those who daily commune with God, letting him breathe his life into their souls, become strong with that secret, hidden strength which preserves them from falling in the day of trial. They have a "vessel" from which to refill the lamp when its little cup of oil is exhausted.

For further thought:
1. In which group should I be included—the "wise" or the "foolish"?
2. What am I doing to "get in shape" spiritually?

To be ready for whatever comes, today I will:

12 APRIL

He saith unto him the third time, Simon, son of Jonas, lovest thou me? Peter was grieved because he said unto him the third time, Lovest thou me? And he said unto him, Lord, thou knowest all things; thou knowest that I love thee. Jesus saith unto him, Feed my sheep.

—John 21:17

Christ has committed to his disciples the work of seeking, winning, and gathering perishing souls. The redemption is divine, but the mediation of it is human. So far as we know, no lost sinner is brought to repentance and faith except through one who already believes. It is the Holy Spirit who draws souls to Christ, yet the Spirit works *through* believers *on* unbelievers. We see thus a hint of our responsibility for the saving of the lost souls whom our soul touches. There are those who will never be saved unless we do our part to save them. Our responsibility is commensurate with our opportunity. Christ wants to pour his grace through us to other lives every day, and we are ready for this most sacred of all ministries only when we are content to be nothing that Christ may be all in all, when we let ourselves be vessels emptied that he may fill them, channels through which his grace may flow.

For further thought:
1. Am I a "channel" Christian?
2. Is there anything in my life to "clog up" the work of Christ?

Today I will:

Finally, all of you, have unity of spirit, sympathy, love of the brethren, a tender heart and a humble mind.

—1 Peter 3:8, RSV

Peter is calling for a spirit here that involves more than mere "unity." If he were a musician he might have used a different word, as the New International Version does here—*harmony.* Mere unity in music could become rather dull—a monotonous unison that wouldn't necessarily grate on the ear, but wouldn't do much to excite us either. But beautiful harmony, the blending of many notes and instruments together, can thrill the soul tremendously. Another example of harmony in the natural world can be seen in a field of multicolored flowers. Here in Texas April is a brilliantly colorful month with bluebonnets, reddish-orange Indian paintbrush, and other varieties of wildflowers blending in a blanket of brilliant variegated color that fills one's vision from horizon to horizon. It is a mixture of color blended by the Master Artist as an illustration of the way he wants his children to work together in harmony—not in mere conformity.

For further thought:
1. Am I a "harmonious" or a "dissonant" Christian?
2. How do my gifts blend in with those of others?

Lord, help me today to "harmonize" better with:

So faith, hope, love abide, these three; but the greatest of these is love.
                              —1 Corinthians 13:13, RSV

The love which comes from God is limitless. This kind of love is measured by what it will do, what it will give, what it will suffer. God so loved the world that he gave—gave his only begotten Son, gave all, withheld nothing. That is the measure of the divine love for us: it loves to the uttermost. If I am Christ's, every energy of my mind, every affection of my heart, every power of my soul, every fiber of my body, every asset of my influence, every penny of my money is Christ's, and all of these are to be used to bless my fellow-men and to make the world better and happier. If I love, I will give and suffer and sacrifice. If I would be like God, I must live to minister, giving my life without reserve to service in Christ's name.

For further thought:
1. To whom do I direct my love?
2. From whom do I seek my love?

To show love today, I will:

All these [gifts] are inspired by one and the same Spirit, who apportions to each one individually as he wills.

—1 Corinthians 12:11, RSV

The greatest men are but fractions of men. No one is endowed with all gifts. Every one has his own particular excellence or ability. No two have precisely the same gifts, and no two are called to fill precisely the same place in life. The lowliest and the humblest in endowments is just as important in his place as the most brilliantly gifted. The great life in God's sight is not the conspicuous one, but the life that fills the place which it was made to fill, and does the work which it was made to do. God asks not great things; he asks only simple faithfulness, the quiet doing of what he allots. God does not measure greatness with the same ruler man does.

J. R. MILLER

For further thought:
1. What are some of the Spirit-inspired "gifts" I have discovered in my life?
2. How am I using them to God's glory in my life today? What are some ways I could make better use of them?

Using my God-given gifts, today I will:

16 APRIL

We who first hoped in Christ have been destined and appointed to life for the praise of his glory.

—Ephesians 1:12, RSV

Should the uncertainty of earthly affairs dampen our lives? No, God does not want us to bring tomorrow's possible clouds to shadow our todays. He does not want us to be unhappy while the sun shines because by-and-by it will be dark. He wants us to live in today and enjoy its blessings and do its work well, though tomorrow may bring tragedy or trauma. How can we? Only by calm, quiet, trustful faith in God and obedience to him at every step. Then no troubled tomorrow can ever bring us harm. When the storm breaks, God will hide under his wings those who have done his will each day. Trusting him all along the way is a measure of our faith and practice.

For further thought:
1. Do I ever let fears about tomorrow cloud up my todays?
2. Do I really believe God is able to watch over me—and do I live that belief?

Today, Lord, I will give my fears to you and:

But I say unto you which hear, Love your enemies, do good to them that hate you, Bless them that curse you, and pray for them which despitefully use you.

—Luke 6:27, 28

Jesus had some clear-cut suggestions as to what we are to do with those who injure us. What are we to do with the wrongs and injustices and injuries inflicted upon us by others if we are not to avenge them? How are these wrongs to be righted and these injuries to be healed? Don't fear the consequences of any wrong done to you. Simply turn the matter over to God and leave it there, and he will work it all out. He will not allow us to be permanently or irreversibly injured by any injustice. Our duty, then, is to bear meekly and patiently the suffering which others may cause us to endure, to treat with love the hand that strikes us, to forgive those who injure us, and to commit all the injustices and inequities of our lives into the hand of the just and righteous God. The oyster's wounds become pearls, and God can bring pearls of spiritual beauty out of the hurts made by human hands in our lives.

For further study:
1. What would happen if I really tried to follow this lifestyle commanded by Jesus?
2. Is there a particular person(s) I should be treating in this fashion?

Today I will:

18 APRIL

Read Psalm 34:11–14
Also see John 14:25–27

Depart from evil, and do good; seek peace, and pursue it.

—Psalm 34:14

Where Christ places us we are to remain; where he sends us we are to go; and in the heat of life's conflicts, surrounded on every side by a host of things which tend to disturb our peace, we are to maintain an unruffled calm and all the tenderness and simplicity of the heart of a little child. That is the problem of life and of loving which Christ sets before us, and which he will help us to solve if we accept him as our teacher. As the tender grass and even sweet flowers live and grow all through the winter under the deep snows, and come forth in the springtime in beauty, so our hearts may remain loving, tender, and joyous through life's fiercest winter under the snows of trial and sorrow—if our pipeline of peace is not clogged with the world's clutter.

For further thought:
1. Am I actively "pursuing peace"?
2. If this peace is the Savior's gift, do I *have* to pursue it?

Lord, help me today to:

May he have dominion from sea to sea, and from the river to the ends of the earth!

—Psalm 72:8, RSV

This psalm of Solomon pictures the reign and kingdom of the Messiah, Jesus Christ. It is no petty or provincial thing that our Lord has undertaken to do in the world. He has projected a kingdom that is to be world-wide. This is the glory of our Christianity. Our God is no tribal deity, but the Father of all mankind. He calls us all to share with him in extending his influence in human life until the last man has heard the gospel and become a Christian— and not only until the last nation or group of men, and the last social institution shall have accepted his rule of love and the order of Christian brotherhood. This will not come about because of man's goodness, but because of God's greatness!

For further thought:
1. What part can I play in the spread of Christ's kingdom?
2. Am I living a life that lifts up the Savior?

As one of God's soldiers today I will:

20 APRIL

Religion that God our Father accepts as pure and faultless is this: to look after orphans and widows in their distress and to keep oneself from being polluted by the world.

—James 1:27, NIV

"Religion" has received a bad name in our modern world—but James here puts it into proper perspective for me. For too long it has suffered by an interpretation which made it, in effect, a constriction of life. Religion has been stated or defined in terms of what must be given up. But it should be stated in terms of the immensity of interest the soul takes on. For religion is the response of our life to the call of the infinite and the eternal, and this in no mere far-off and abstract sense, but in its most immediate and concrete realization. Common things take on a new light, and nothing in the world or out of it is alien to the soul who hears and heeds the call of Christ. Ministering to "orphans and widows" is an easily recognizable process—and keeping "oneself unstained from the world" (RSV) is equally clearcut. If I cannot do these duties, then I am missing the best in life.

For further thought:

1. What is the world's definition of "being religious"?
2. How would I describe being truly religious in practical terms?

As an expression of my "religion" today I will:

Let us consider how to stir up one another to love and good works, not neglecting to meet together, as is the habit of some, encouraging one another and all the more as you see the Day drawing near.
—Hebrews 10:24, 25, RSV

God's presence is particularly felt in his house. God's Spirit is everywhere, but he reveals himself to our hearts with special graciousness in the place set apart for divine worship. It is not strange that this is so. A congregation singing his praises, reading his Word, thinking together upon some theme of the spiritual life and offering a common prayer, carries a blessing to each individual worshiper which no one can quite attain in solitude. It is important that we prepare our hearts in advance by quieting our anxieties and meditating upon the love of God, so we may enter into his gates with thanksgiving and into his courts with praise (see Ps. 100:4).

For further thought:
1. What is my usual attitude in the house of God?
2. Do I look forward to the worship experience—or is it a "chore" or "duty"?

To put "feet on my faith" today I will:

22 APRIL

Read Psalm 40:11-17

As for me, I am poor and needy; but the Lord takes thought for me.
Thou art my help and my deliverer; do not tarry, oh my God!
—Psalm 40:17, RSV

How grateful I should be that "the Lord takes thought for me"! God's boundless and unstinting grace is mine each day of my life—and I am seldom, if ever, aware of it. His mercy reaches out to the farthest soul—and it reaches down to my deepest sin. No one in all the world, except the Lord Jesus himself, was ever good enough not to need this overflow from the heart of God. And even he once cried out, "My God, my God, why hast thou forsaken me?" Even saints feel the need for just as much of God's mercy as prodigals pray for. And, praise God, not a one of us, no matter how wayward, is beyond Christ's love. He can and will lead us back to the Father whose tender mercy more than equals our guilt.

For further consideration:
1. Do I sometimes limit God's ministry of mercy to me by my unbelief?
2. How can I become more of a channel of God's mercy to those around me?

Knowing God "takes thought for me," today I will:

The people of Israel said to the Lord, "We have sinned; do to us whatever seems good to thee, only deliver us, we pray thee, this day."
—Judges 10:15, RSV

Any seasoned soldier will tell you that battles are not won by a series of tactics set out in advance. Rather, the successful soldier knows that battles are won by the consistent accomplishment of daily objectives, each in its order. In the discipline of our souls it seems enough if we can meet the test of one day at a time. Praying for tomorrow and its need too often takes our attention away from the task at hand, and if this habit of anticipatory prayer be too long indulged, our spiritual life becomes a mere daydream, a flight of fancy. Our prayer should keep today with its need in the foreground, for the present is big with destiny.

For further thought:
1. Is it possible to be so concerned for tomorrow that I miss God's best for me today?
2. What specific situations am I facing today for which I need the Lord's help and guidance?

Today, Lord, help me to see this day in perspective. Today I want to:

As it is, I rejoice, not because you were grieved, but because you were grieved into repenting; for you felt a godly grief, so that you have suffered no loss through us.

—2 Corinthians 7:9, RSV

To repent is not simply to be sorry for our wrongdoing, though sorrow and regret are essential to repentance. It is rather to take a new point of view from which our sin will not only be regretted but positively hated. William Mackergo Taylor wrote, "True repentance hates the sin, and not merely the penalty; and it hates the sin most of all because it has discovered and felt God's love." Repentance implies a changed mind, a right-about-face for our soul, a new outlook. Nor is it an act that we accomplish once and for all at the beginning of our Christian life. Rather, it is a spiritual attitude we carry continually with us as a habit of the soul, whereby we make it possible for Christ to repair and redeem us when we fall into temptation.

For further thought:
1. Was repentance a factor in my first coming to Christ?
2. Is there anything in my life now that needs to be repented of?

Today I'm sorry that I:

Whom have I in heaven but thee? And there is nothing upon earth that I desire besides thee.

—Psalm 73:25, RSV

These words from the psalmist Asaph point up a spiritual truth I don't often think about: God is to be adored, but he is also to be used. Merely to worship him in all of his greatness and holiness is not to please him fully. He wants me to draw upon him, to treat him as an asset of my workaday world, and as a priceless possession. I live in him; but he also lives in me, to bring to my soul the power of his own infinite life. To possess him is to possess all things, and to have power to obtain my noblest goals and purposes.

For further thought:
1. Am I living as though God were my most precious possession?
2. What does it mean to "use" God?

Since God is "in my corner," today I will:

If you are willing and obedient, you shall eat the good of the land.
—Isaiah 1:19, RSV

There is a spiritual principle that is often missed here in Isaiah because we become so wrapped up in the majestic message of verse 18: "Come now, let us reason together, says the Lord: though your sins are like scarlet, they shall be as white as snow; though they are red like crimson, they shall become like wool" (RSV). Way back in Deuteronomy 30:15, 16, the Lord God of Isaiah introduced this concept of obedience as the spiritual "secret of success": "See, I have set before you this day life and good, death and evil. If you obey the commandments of the Lord your God which I command you this day, by loving the Lord your God, by walking in his ways, and by keeping his commandments and his statutes and his ordinances, then you shall live and multiply, and the Lord your God will bless you in the land you are entering..." (RSV). God's side of the agreement is already "etched in stone." My part of the agreement is a simple "yes" or "no" to his commandment to "love... walk in... and keep" his laws. With Joshua of old, I must choose this day whom I will serve. Will I follow God or the world?

For further thought:

1. Is my obedience "willing" or reluctant?
2. How do I make my choices—by myself or by prayer?

Today I will:

Behold, we count them happy which endure. Ye have heard of the patience of Job, and have seen the end of the Lord; that the Lord is very pitiful, and of tender mercy [compassionate and merciful— RSV].

—James 5:11

The spiritual life needs opposition to bring out its best development. It flourishes most luxuriantly in adverse circumstances. The very temptations which make our life one unceasing warfare train us to become true soldiers of Christ. The hardnesses of our experiences, which seem to us to be more than we can possibly endure, make the very school of life for us in which we learn our best lessons and grow into whatever beauty and Christlikeness of character we attain.

For further thought:
1. Someone has said, "Opposition is a means of grace." What does that mean?
2. What am I enduring right now that will help me grow in grace?

Today I will:

28 APRIL

Is any among you suffering? Let him pray. Is any cheerful? Let him sing praise.

—James 5:13, RSV

It is blessedly possible to master misfortune. An English prisoner, suffering solitary confinement, was cheered for one hour each day by a little spot of sunshine which shone upon his dungeon wall. Through a grating high up the sun's rays streamed down into his cell for a short time. He found on his floor an old nail and a stone, and with these rude implements he cut upon the wall while the sunlight shone upon it a rough image of the Christ upon his cross. Thus he mastered his misfortune, getting blessing out of it.

His experience has a lesson for us all. Whatever the persecution that builds its prison walls round us, we must never let despair lay its chilly hand upon us or yield to gloom. There is no dungeon so deep and dark but down into its chilling gloom the rays of God's love can stream and form some new beauty on my soul. I must carve on the wall of my heart the image of the Christ. If I master my misfortune, I can make it yield blessing. Conquered calamity becomes a helper, and leaves beauty on the soul; but let a trouble master us, and it leaves a lasting scar upon our life.

For further thought:
1. Do I know what it means to suffer?
2. What kind of suffering am I called upon to endure?

In the light of what I am learning through suffering today I will:

As obedient children, do not be conformed to the passions of your former ignorance, but as he who called you is holy, be holy yourselves in all your conduct; since it is written, "You shall be holy, for I am holy."

—1 Peter 1:14–16, RSV

These words from the apostle Peter point up a spiritual truth of which I need to be reminded. "As obedient children," our lives are to be so surrendered to him that the arbitrary and artificial division between sacred and secular is nonexistent. As Peter says, God's plan is, "You shall be holy, for I am holy."—"As he who called you is holy, be holy yourselves in all your conduct." That means that God goes with me into my workaday world as well as into my worship experience. He's to be part of my pain as well as my pleasure. If I can't take him with me on Saturday night, I shouldn't expect him to be waiting for me on the church steps Sunday morning. The secret lies in surrender to the Holy Spirit of God who can go with me *everywhere,* infilling my life with spiritual power sufficient to let me "climb every mountain."

For further thought:
1. Are there things from my "former" life which hinder my spiritual progress today?
2. Are there aspects of my life into which I would hesitate to let God go with me? What should being called to be "holy" change about my life?
3. How can I be "holy" without being "holier than thou"?

Today I will:

30 APRIL

Read 1 Peter 5:6–11

Cast all your anxieties on him, for he cares about you.
—1 Peter 5:7, RSV

Centuries ago the philosopher Seneca said, "The mind that is anxious is miserable." About the same time, Peter was saying much the same thing, but from a totally different perspective—for he knew the Source and the Sender of inner peace, Jesus Christ. What we need to do is to shift our anxieties along with our sins over to the One who "cares" and can give us abundant life. Then we can discover the peace and provision he has to give us as we begin walking the path of surrender to him who holds our future in his caring and compassionate hands.

For further thought:
1. Am I able *consistently* to do as Peter urges here?
2. If not, why not?

Today I will turn over:

What shall I say then? Is the law sin? God forbid. Nay, I had not known sin, but by the law; for I had not known lust, except the law had said, Thou shalt not covet.

—Romans 7:7

What is sin? This chapter is a great story of a tragedy, the awful power of sin. The suggestions that it is an infirmity, a form of heredity, or mere selfishness do not satisfy the soul's real sense of guilt, however plausible they are as theories. They all leave God out of the picture. We may excuse others, but we cannot lighten our own sense of responsibility. It is revolt against God and it leads to loss of life. Education and environment will not remove its power; they may only change the place of emphasis. I thank God through Jesus Christ, Christ did not come to describe sin but to destroy it.

J. H. JOWETT (1863–1923)

For further thought:

1. As I look at my life, where am I weakest in terms of yielding to my sinful impulses?
2. What are the ways I tend to disguise my tendency to fall into a certain type of sin?

Today I will:

Remember not the sins of my youth, nor my transgressions; according to thy mercy remember thou me for goodness' sake, O Lord.

—Psalm 25:7

We need to know that our sins are forgiven. And how shall we know this? By feeling that we have peace with God—by feeling that we are able so to trust in the divine compassion and infinite tenderness of our Father, as to arise and go to him, whenever we commit sin, and say at once to him, "Father, I have sinned; forgive me." To know that we are forgiven, it is only necessary to look at our Father's love till it sinks into our heart, to open our soul to him till he shall pour his love into it; to wait on him till we find peace, till our conscience no longer torments us, till the weight of responsibility ceases to be an oppressive burden to us, till we can feel that our sins, great as they are, cannot keep us away from our Heavenly Father.

J. F. CLARKE (1810–1888)

For further thought:
1. Have I found peace with God in confessing my sin to him?
2. If not, is it because I am holding something back—or perhaps have failed to see something as sin?

Lord, help me today to:

Watch therefore—for you do not know when the master of the house will come, in the evening, or at midnight, or at cockcrow, or in the morning.

—Mark 13:35, RSV

All Christ wants from any of us is what we have the ability to do. He lays no impossible assignments on us. He accepts our homeliest, poorest gifts or services if they are indeed our best and if true love to him consecrates and sanctifies them. We need to be concerned for but two things—that we always do our best, and that we do what we do through love for Christ. If we are faithful up to the measure of our ability and opportunity, and if love sanctifies what we do, we are sure of our Lord's approval. But we should never offer less than the best that we can do; to do so is to be disloyal to our Lord and disloyal to our own soul.

For further thought:
1. Am I looking forward to my Lord's return?
2. Am I faithfully serving him today, to the very best of my ability?

Giving it my best effort, today I will:

4 MAY

He that loveth not knoweth not God; for God is love.

—1 John 4:8

Whatever makes us forget ourselves and think of others lifts us upward. This is one reason that God permits suffering. We would never know the best and richest of human love if there were no pain, no distress, no appeal of grief or of need. The deepest and holiest of mother-love would never be brought out if the child never suffered. The same is true of God's love. God would have loved his children unfallen just as much as he loves them fallen, but the world would never have known so much of God's love had not man fallen. Our terrible need called out all that was richest, holiest, and most divine in our Father's heart. If no night ever came, we would never know there are stars. Darkness is a revealer.

For further thought:
1. How much do I know about God's love personally?
2. Am I sharing that love with others—or hoarding it?

As a lover of God and my fellow-man, today I will:

The Lord is near to all who call upon him, to all who call upon him in truth. He fulfils the desire of all who fear him, he also hears their cry, and saves them.

—Psalm 145:18, 19, RSV

God himself is his own best gift! Enlarge your desires and your prayers. Do not ask merely for mercies and favors and common gifts. Do not ask God merely to give you bread, and health, and home, and friends, and prosperity; or, rising yet a step higher, do not content yourself with asking for grace to help in temptation, or for strength to fill up your weakness, or for wisdom to guide you in perplexity, or for holiness and purity and power. Ask for God himself, and then open your heart to receive him. If you have God, you have all other gifts and blessings in him. And it is himself that God is willing to give for the asking, not merely the favors and benefits that his hand dispenses. Ask most largely.

J. R. MILLER (1840–1912)

For further thought:
1. Am I "asking largely" when I pray?
2. Am I praying in an attitude of praise?
3. What should I be asking for right now?

Lord, my "large" prayer today is that you will:

6 MAY

One thing have I asked of the Lord, that will I seek after; that I may dwell in the house of the Lord all the days of my life, to behold the beauty of the Lord, and to inquire in his temple.

—Psalm 27:4, RSV

God give us visions of spiritual beauty that we may turn them into realities in common life. All our heavenward aspirations we should bring down and work into acts. All our longings and desires we should make true in experiences. Every day's Bible text taken into the heart should shine forth tomorrow in some new touch of spiritual beauty. As the look of the face in the camera is held there, so every time Christ looks in upon our souls, even for an instant, some impression of his features should become fixed there, and remain as part of our own spiritual beauty. So in all our life the words of Christ we hear, the lessons we are taught, and the holy influences that touch our souls, should enter into our very being and reappear in disposition, character, deeds.

J. R. MILLER (1840–1912)

For further thought:
1. Has Christ "looked into" my life today?
2. What word of his has entered my being?

Since my life is an open book to God, today I will:

Why do you look at the speck of sawdust in your brother's eye and pay no attention to the plank in your own eye?

—Luke 6:41, NIV

No doubt it is easier to see other people's faults than our own. Many of us are troubled more about the way our neighbors live than we are with our own shortcomings. We show a greater feeling of responsibility for the acts and misdeeds of others than for our own.

Now, the truth is, every one of us must bear his own burden. I shall not be called to answer at God's bar for my neighbor's idle words, sinful acts, and neglect of duty. But there is one person for whose every act, word, disposition, and feeling I shall have to give an account—and that is myself. I had better train myself therefore, to keep close, minute, incessant, and conscientious watch over my own life. I had better give less attention to my neighbor's mistakes, foibles, and failures, and more to my own. Most of us would find little time for looking after other people's faults if we gave strict attention to our own. Besides, seeing and knowing our own defects would make us more charitable concerning those of others.

For further thought:
1. What is the "plank" in my eye today?
2. What is the "speck" I am seeing in someone else's eye?

As I look deep into my own heart, today I will:

8 MAY

Beloved, if God so loved us, we also ought to love one another.
                                            —1 John 4:11, RSV

We should learn to look at the faults of others only through love's eyes, with charity, patience, and compassion. We do not know the secret history of the lives of others about us. We do not know what piercing sorrows have produced the scars which we see in people's souls. We do not know the pains and trials which make life hard to many with whom we are tempted to be impatient. If we knew all the secret burdens and the heart-wounds which many carry hidden beneath their smiling faces, we would be patient and gentle with all men.

J. R. MILLER (1840–1912)

For further thought:
1. Is there someone in my life with whom I need to be especially "patient and gentle"?
2. What limits does God put on his love?

Lord, help me today to especially love:

I have been crucified with Christ; it is no longer I who live, but Christ who lives in me; and the life I now live in the flesh I live by faith in the Son of God, who loved me and gave himself for me.
—Galatians 2:20, RSV

Paul here is describing the life that wins. We can win others to Christ only by being Christ to them, by showing them Christ in us, by living so that they may be attracted to Christ and may learn to admire and to love him by what they see of him in us. One of the most effective ways of winning souls is through beautiful, gentle, Christlike living. Eloquent persuasion by a preacher is powerful with sinners only insofar as the preacher's life is consistent with his words. Preaching without love in the life is only empty clatter. But where deep, true love, the love of Christ, is, the plainest, humblest words become eloquent and mighty. Is my life a mirror of that love?

For further thought:
1. Is there someone I know whom I am to "win" by the way I live?
2. Am I guilty of preaching without practicing?

Today I want "to be Christ" to:

10 MAY

For we have not a high priest who is unable to sympathize with our weaknesses, but one who in every respect has been tempted as we are, yet without sin.

—Hebrews 4:15, RSV

Life is God's strange school for his children. No book, no university, can teach me the divine art of sympathy. I must be sorely tempted myself before I can understand what others suffer in their temptations. I must experience sorrow myself in some form before I can be a real and true comforter to others in their times of sorrow. I must walk through the deep valley myself before I can be a guide to others in the same shadowy places. I must feel the strain and carry the burden and endure the struggle myself, and then I can be touched with the feeling of sympathy or can give help to others in life's stress and extremity. So I see here one compensation of suffering: it fits me in a larger sense for being a helper of others.

For further thought:
1. What have been my "deep places"?
2. What have I learned there?
3. Whom can I help with what I have learned?

Out of my "deep places" I will reach out to:

The sacrifices of God are a broken spirit: a broken and a contrite heart, O God, thou wilt not despise.

—Psalm 51:17

When it is the one ruling, never-ceasing desire of our hearts that God may be the beginning and end, the reason and motive, the rule and measure, of our doing or not doing, from morning to night; then everywhere, whether speaking or silent, whether inwardly or outwardly employed, we are equally offered up to the eternal Spirit, have our life in Him and from Him, and are united to Him by that Spirit of Prayer which is the comfort, the support, the strength and security of the soul, travelling, by the help of God, through the vanity of time into riches of eternity. Let us have no thought or care, but how to be wholly His devoted instruments; everywhere and in everything, His adoring, joyful and thankful servants.

WILLIAM LAW (1686–1761)

For further thought:
1. As I read the New Testament passage relating the parables of the treasure in the field and the pearl of great price, can I apply them to the value of a broken and submissive spirit?
2. Do I need my spirit "broken" about something in my life right now? What issues am I most proud and stubborn about? Why is it so hard to "give in"?

Lord, help me keep a contrite heart today as I:

And if any man say aught unto you, ye shall say, The Lord hath need of them, and straightway he will send them.

—Matthew 21:3

J. R. Miller (1840–1912) takes an interesting view of this entire passage: "There seems to have been no formal request of the owner for the use of the colt. Jesus sent his disciples to take it by divine authority. So then the Lord has a right to anything we have. No property right that we can get takes the title out of his hands. We talk about our possessions as if they were ours indeed. Nothing is really ours save as lent to us by the Lord to be used for him."

Is this the way I view my possessions—as though they rightfully belong to God and that I am just a steward of the things he has entrusted to me? It is strange that we never hear any more about this man. Did he become a follower of Jesus? He is an "unsung hero" whose story seems to end here, as does the story of so many of us. But his commitment to the cause of Christ rings clear in this cameo performance. How is my performance?

For further thought:
1. Am I holding on to some possession I need to give to God?
2. How would I react if someone, a stranger to me, came to me and asked for one of my prized possessions, saying, "The Lord hath need of them"?

Lord, today I give you:

In all these things we are more than conquerors through him who loved us.

—Romans 8:37, RSV

J. Wilbur Chapman (1859–1918) told this story: "A farmer allowed his old, worn-out, blind horse to wander about the premises with all freedom. One night the old horse fell into an abandoned well. It was decided that, since the well was useless and the horse was useless, it would be convenient to fill the well and bury the horse with the same operation. But the earth that was shoveled in to cover up the horse made a good foundation for his feet, and he kept on top of it all the time. When the well was filled to the level of the ground, the old horse walked away to graze on the meadow." This is a parable representing the effect of opposition upon the Christian. "If God be for us, who can be against us?"

For further consideration:
1. Do I handle opposition and persecution like the horse did?
2. What is the secret of the overcoming life according to today's verse?

Lord, today I want to conquer:

14 MAY

In whom ye also are builded together for an habitation of God through the Spirit.

—Ephesians 2:22

Phillips Brooks (1835–1893) used these words to describe the process of building: "Slowly, through all the universe, that temple of God is being built. Wherever, in any world, a soul, by free-willed obedience, catches the fire of God's likeness, it is set into the growing walls, a living stone. When, in your hard fight, in your tiresome drudgery, or in your terrible temptation, you catch the purpose of your being, and give yourself to God, and so give Him the chance to give Himself to you, your life, a living stone, is taken up and set into that growing wall. Wherever souls are being tried and ripened, in whatever commonplace and homely ways—there God is hewing out the pillars for his temple. Oh, if the stone can only have some vision of the temple of which it is to be a part forever, what patience must fill it as it feels the blows of the hammer, and knows that success for it is simply to let itself be wrought into what shape the Master wills."

For further thought:
1. Revelation 3:12 says, "Him that overcometh will I make a pillar in the temple of my God." Am I overcoming?
2. God has the "big picture" in mind at all times. Have I had a glimpse of it?

Lord, today take my life and:

You then, my son, be strong in the grace that is in Christ Jesus.
—2 Timothy 2:1, RSV

There is a blessing in struggle. The daily temptations which make every true life such a painful conflict from beginning to end bring us constant opportunities for growth of character. Not to struggle is not to grow strong. The soldier's art can be learned and the soldier's honors can be won only on the field of battle. If you would grow into the beauty of the Master, you must accept the conflicts and fight the battles. You can have life easy, if you will, by declining every struggle, but you will then get little out of life that is truly noble and noteworthy. The best things all lie beyond some battlefield; you must fight your way across the field to get them. Heaven is only for those who overcome. None get the crown without the conflict save those who are called home in infancy and early childhood. As the hymn writer says, "Sure I must fight if I would reign."

For further thought:
1. What in my life right now is a "growing experience"?
2. What should I be learning from it?

Today I want to win by:

16 MAY

Thou dost show me the path of life; in thy presence there is fulness of joy, in thy right hand are pleasures for evermore.

—Psalm 16:11, RSV

Many a great battle is won or lost based on what is held in reserve. The struggle is perfectly balanced, and victory is uncertain. Then one side or the other brings up its reserve, and instantly the question is settled. Life's battles are often determined in like manner—by the reserve or the absence of a reserve. No life is a level experience from cradle to grave. The days are not all bright. The course is not all smooth. The experiences are not all easy. We must all be attacked by temptations and by spiritual foes. Victory can be gained only if we have reserves of resistance to call into action. We must all stand before tasks and duties which will overwhelm our ability if we have no more strength to draw on than we have been using in the common duties of the common days. Blessed are they who have learned to draw on the infinite resources of divine strength; with the fulness of God as reserve they can never fail.

For further thought:
1. Am I submitting myself to Christ's "fulness"?
2. In what area of my struggle do I need his fulness right now?

Lord, today I open my life to you to:

As for what fell among the thorns, they are those who hear, but as they go on their way they are choked by the cares and riches and pleasures of life, and their fruit does not mature.

—Luke 8:14, RSV

Anything allowed in the heart which is contrary to the will of God, let it seem ever so insignificant, or be ever so deeply hidden, will cause us to fall before our enemies. Any root of bitterness cherished toward another, any self-seeking, any harsh judgments indulged in, any slackness in obeying the voice of God, any doubtful habits or surroundings, any one of these things will effectually cripple and paralyze our spiritual life. I believe our blessed Guide, the indwelling Holy Spirit, is always secretly discovering those things to us by continual little twinges and pangs of conscience, so that we are left without excuse.

HANNAH WHITALL SMITH (1832–1911)

For further thought:
1. According to the parable of the sower (vv. 4–8), what kind of soil am I?
2. Are there any "thorns" in my life that keep me from producing the "fruit that matures"?

Because I want to bear good fruit, today I want to rid my life of:

Being confident of this very thing, that he which hath begun a good work in you will perform it until the day of Jesus Christ.

—Philippians 1:6

If any sincere Christian cast himself with his whole will upon the Divine Presence which dwells within him, he shall be kept safe unto the end. What is it that makes us unable to persevere? Is it want of strength? By no means. We have with us the strength of the Holy Spirit. When did we ever set ourselves sincerely to any work according to the will of God, and fail for want of strength? It was not that strength failed the will, but that the will failed first. If we could but embrace the Divine will with the whole love of ours; cleaving to it, and holding fast by it, we should be borne along as upon "the river of the water of life." We open only certain chambers of our will to the influence of the Divine will. We are afraid of being wholly absorbed into it. And yet, if we would have peace, we must be altogether united to him.

H. E. MANNING (1808–1892)

For further thought:

1. Is Christ at home in my heart? (Editor's Note: A good book to read in connection with this meditation is *My Heart Christ's Home* by Robert Boyd Munger.)
2. What rooms in my heart have I closed off to him?

Lord, I want to open the following rooms of my heart to you:

I appeal to you therefore, brethren, by the mercies of God, to present your bodies as a living sacrifice, holy and acceptable to God.... Do not be conformed to this world but be transformed by the renewal of your mind, that you may prove what is the will of God, what is good and acceptable and perfect.

—Romans 12:1, 2, RSV

Our heart is to be Christ's kingdom. Religion is not an art or a science. It is not the mere learning and following of a set of rules. It is the growth of Christlikeness in the heart, spreading out into the whole being. It is the setting up of the kingdom of heaven within us. This kingdom in one's heart is the rule and authority of Christ, owned and recognized there at the very fount of life. It is the rule of love—"the love of Christ constraineth us" (2 Cor. 5:14). Paul goes even further and speaks of it as a new incarnation: "Christ liveth in me" (Gal. 2:20). A Christian life is therefore really the personal reign of Christ in the heart of everyone who accepts him. The process is slow and it is not complete till the believer passes into heaven. All earthly Christian life is therefore a learning to be Christian. We should devote ourselves to our King, placing heart, soul, will, and mind into complete subjection to Christ.

For further thought:
1. What do I do now that is "good and acceptable" in motive?
2. If "Christ liveth in me," what should I be doing right now?

Lord, remove from my heart:

O Lord, thou hast searched me and known me.

—Psalm 139:1

God looks upon each of us as individuals. We come into this world one by one. We live in a sense alone with our own personal responsibilities. We die one by one. As individuals, not as crowds, must we stand before God. My destiny will not depend on any chance of the moment; I am fixing it myself in my choices and acts, in my habits and life. My own faith and obedience must weave the garment of beauty for my life.

For further thought:
1. Am I living my life as if God knows me?
2. Am I aware of any tasks for the Lord only I can do? What does this tell me about my importance in God's eyes?
3. What would I begin to do if I really believed that God knows me?

Because you "know" me, Lord, help me to:

And she called the name of the Lord that spake unto her, Thou God seest me: for she said, Have I also here looked after him that seeth me?

—Genesis 16:13

There is never a moment, nor any experience, in the life of an authentic Christian, from the heart of which a prayer may not instantly be sent up to God. And help will instantly come. God is not off in some remote heaven. He is not away at the top of the tall steep life-ladder, looking down upon us in disinterested calm, watching us as we struggle upward in pain and tears. He is with each one of us on every part of the way. His promise of his presence is an eternal present tense—"I *am* with thee." So "Thou God seest me" becomes to the believer a most cheering and inspiring assurance. We are never out of God's sight for a moment. His eye watches each one of us continually, and his heart is in his eye. He comes instantly to our help and deliverance when we are in any need or danger.

For further thought:
1. Does the fact that "Thou God seest me" frighten or calm me?
2. Are there some things about my lifestyle I would rather God not see?

Because you "see" me, Lord, help me to:

22 MAY

Daniel answered and said, Blessed be the name of God for ever and ever: for wisdom and might are his.

—Daniel 2:20

Think of all the magnificent powers God has put into these lives of ours. He has given us minds to think with, to reason, to imagine, to roam amid the stars, to wander into the very borders of infinity, to climb the golden stairs of faith even into the midst of heaven's brightness. He has given us hearts to feel, to suffer, to rejoice, to love. He has put into our beings the possibilities of the noblest achievements and the loftiest attainments. Oh, what a shame it is for one born to live in immortal glory, called to be a child of God, to become like the Son of God, yet to be content with a poor earthly life and to live without reaching up toward God and heaven!

J. R. MILLER (1840–1912)

For further thought:
1. Am I following Daniel's example of devotion to God?
2. Am I content with less than God's best for me?

Because God's wisdom and might are mine, today I will:

I saw in the night visions, and behold with the clouds of heaven there came one like a son of man and he came to the Ancient of Days and was presented before him.

—Daniel 7:13, RSV

Daniel is describing future events here. "The Ancient of Days" is God himself, the One whose kingdom will be eternal and to whom all the nations of the world will ultimately be subservient. Daniel's vision allowed him to see in advance the crumbling kingdoms of our day. He also saw that, upon the ruins of man's failure, Christ would come again to set up his kingdom. Sometimes we humans must learn *we cannot* before we can accept the fact that *God can!* The One described in verses 13 and 14 is the risen Lord, and some day he *will* reign in the only Kingdom that cannot be destroyed.

For further consideration:
1. Do I live my life in the light of Jesus' soon return?
2. Why should I worry about the future if God is in charge?

In full awareness of God's greatness, today I will:

Give ear to my words, O Lord, consider my meditation. Hearken unto the voice of my cry, my King, and my God: for unto thee will I pray.
—Psalm 5:1, 2

True prayer is earnest, not tiring nor fainting. It takes every burden to God—the small and the large alike. It is submissive, referring all to the Father's will. Its answer may not come in the direct granting of the request we make, but may come instead in increased grace and strength that enables us to keep the burden and yet rejoice. Lying at our Father's feet in the time of our trials and tears, we learn obedience, and our sobs end in praises, our struggles in acquiescence, Our tears are dried, and we rise victorious—not getting our own way, but glad and happy and peaceful in God's way.

For further thought:
1. Are my prayers as specific as this one of David's?
2. What kind of answers do my prayers receive?

Lord, today I pray:

There is no fear in love. But perfect love drives out fear, because fear has to do with punishment. A man who fears is not made perfect in love.

—1 John 4:18, NIV

The uncertainty of the present day has instilled into our world an almost inherent fear of the future. Chaos and confusion are common on every continent. The incidence of mental breakdown is increasing, and more and more people are experiencing facing loneliness and alienation in a world grown suddenly smaller and more vulnerable. In such a world only the Christian, anchored in the love of God, can say with clarity and conviction, "There is no fear in love!" In this uncertain world, we have the only assurance for the future. Only we can confidently look ahead to a place where we have an eternal future without fear. This gives us the inner freedom, regardless of outward circumstances, to live our lives unfettered by the many fears that would cripple and crush us.

For further thought:
1. What am I afraid of?
2. Is God able to overcome this?

Because I am loved, today I will:

26 MAY

Now our Lord Jesus Christ himself, and God, even our Father, which hath loved us, and hath given us everlasting consolation and good hope through grace, Comfort your hearts, and stablish you in every good word and work.

—2 Thessalonians 2:16,17

God's love is unchanging. Human love may change. The friendship of last year can grow cold. The gentleness of yesterday can turn to severity. But it is never this way with God's love. It is eternal. Our experience of it may be variable, but there is no variableness in the love. Our lives may change, our consciousness of his love may fade out; but the love clings forever, the gentleness of God abides eternal. "For the mountains shall depart, and the hills be removed; but my kindness shall not depart from thee, neither shall the covenant of my peace be removed, saith the Lord that hath mercy on thee" (Isa. 54:10).

For further thought:

1. In what way(s) is Jesus the manifestation of God's love to me?
2. In what way(s) is God's love unlike human love?

In the light of God's love, today I will:

For as high as the heavens are above the earth, so great is his love for those who fear him.

—Psalm 103:11, NIV

God's greatest attribute is not his power, though it is omniscience; not his glory, though it is burning majesty: it is his love. He is greatest as he blesses and serves. The brightest hour in Christ's life was not the hour of his transfiguration, or of his miracle working, or of his sublime teaching, but the hour when he hung in darkness on his cross. Then it was that his love shone out most revealingly. We need to remember for ourselves that the greatest thing in the world is love—that serving is the path to highest honor.

For further thought:
1. What thoughts run through my mind as I read Psalm 103:11?
2. If God so loved me, how ought I to love him—and those of his children whom I see during the day?

Lord, I sense that you are telling me to love:

Not that I complain of want; for I have learned, in whatever state I am, to be content.

—Philippians 4:11, RSV

Paul is opening his heart here to share a conviction that he has voiced elsewhere to his spiritual son, Timothy (1 Tim. 6:6). He has learned that the secret of contentment does not lie in material possessions or advantageous circumstances. Contentment grows out of inner peace and a close walk with Christ, the only Source of this peace. As the writer to the Hebrews counsels us, "Keep your life from love of money, and be content with what you have; for he has said, 'I will never fail you nor forsake you.' Hence we can confidently say, 'The Lord is my helper, I will not be afraid; what can man do to me?'" (13:5–6, RSV). With confidence in a Savior like that, how can we help but be content?

For further thought:
1. Am I guilty of discontent?
2. Am I looking in the wrong places for my security?

Lord, help me to learn a lesson here from Paul—and make me content wherever I am and whatever my circumstances. Today I will:

He is the head of the body, the church: who is the beginning, the first born from the dead; that in all things he might have the preeminence.
—Colossians 1:18

What power this passage implies on the part of Christ, the very incarnation of God himself. I wonder if I really realize what that power can do. There is an account coming out of the annals of medical history which illustrates this power to me.

A man had somehow driven a small section of a broken needle into his eye and subsequent efforts to remove that irritating item had merely driven it deeper into the sensitive inner surfaces of the organ. Then a young doctor came up with a new and unorthodox way to handle the problem. Instead of probing for the foreign object, he brought a small but powerful magnet close to the surface of the eyeball and the metal needle was slowly and almost painlessly lifted out of the eye to the waiting surface of the magnet.

That's a tiny example of the tremendous attraction of Christ— his power to lift out of my life (as a sinner separated from him) those sources of sinful irritation that plague and trouble me. Thus he can give me a new life of freedom and accessibility to him.

For further thought:
1. Is Christ preeminent in my life?
2. Is there something there that his magnet needs to lift out?

Lord, today I turn over to you my:

Blessed is the nation whose God is the Lord, the people whom he has chosen as his heritage!

—Psalm 33:12, RSV

We do not always remember, as we enjoy our national blessings and comforts, what they cost those who won them for us, and those who have conserved them and passed them down to us. We plant flowers on the graves of our soldiers who fell, and we retell in speech and print their heroic deeds. This is all well. We should never let the gratitude die out of our hearts as we think of the blood shed in saving our country. But gratitude is not enough. This redeemed country is a sacred trust in our hands. We are now the conservators of its glory, and we have more to do than sing the praises of its dead heroes and soldiers. There are battles yet to fight—battles for national honor, for righteousness, for truth. We must raise up our grand flag in the face of all enemies. While we honor the memory of those who died in patriotic and holy war, let us ourselves be worthy soldiers in the great moral war that never ceases, and patriots loving country more than party, and truth and righteousness more than political preferment and reward.

For further thought:
1. Do I take my country and its blessings for granted?
2. What can I do personally to deepen the spiritual commitment of myself and those in my circle of influence?

Because I have been blessed by God, today I will:

In all thy ways acknowledge him, and he shall direct thy paths.
—Proverbs 3:6

What does it mean to "acknowledge" God in all our ways? Do we make much of God in our lives? Is God really important to us in conscious personal experience? Are we not prone to make plans and carry them out without once consulting him? True, we talk to him about our souls and about our spiritual affairs, but we do not speak to him about our daily work, our trials, our perplexities, our weekday life. We are not to shut God out of any part of our lives. If we would be able to handle all that lies before us, we need something besides human nature, even at its best. We must get our little lives so attached to God's life that we can draw from his fulness in every time of need.

For further thought:
1. What am I "making" of God in my life—is he Leader or left out?
2. Is there any area of my life where he is not Lord?

Today, to rectify the vacuum in my life, I will:

1 JUNE

Read Galatians 5:22–26

But I am like a green olive tree in the house of God: I trust in the mercy of God for ever and ever.

—Psalm 62:8

The olive is crushed into oil, and the oil is used for soothing and supplying joints and flesh, for nourishing and sustaining the body as food, for illuminating darkness as oil in the lamp. And these three things are the things for which we Christian people have received all our gentleness, and all our beauty, and all our strength—that we may give other people light, that we may be the means of conveying to other people nourishment, that we may move gently in the world as lubricating, sweetening, soothing influences—not irritating or provoking, not leading to strife or alienation. The question, after all, is this: Does anybody gather fruit off us, and would anybody call us "trees of righteousness, the planting of the Lord, that He may be glorified"? May we all open our hearts for the dew from heaven, and then use it to produce in ourselves... fruitfulness!

ALEXANDER MACLAREN (1826–1910)

For further thought:

1. When people and pressures "squeeze" me what comes out?
2. What is the predominant "fruit" in my life?

Today I want to evidence _____ **toward:**

*He that loveth not his brother whom he hath seen, how can he love
God whom he hath not seen?*

—1 John 4:20

It requires far more of the constraining love of Christ to love our
cousins and neighbors as members of the heavenly family, than to
feel the heart warm to our suffering brethren in Tuscany or
Madeira. To love the whole church is one thing; to love—that is, to
delight in the graces and veil the defects of—the person who misunderstood me and opposed my plans yesterday, whose peculiar
infirmities grate on my most sensitive feelings, or whose natural
faults are precisely those from which my natural character most
revolts, is quite another.

ELIZABETH CHARLES (1827–1896)

For further thought:
1. Who in my immediate circle "bugs" me?
2. How can I overcome that animosity and love that person
   as Christ would have me do?

Lord, today help me to love:

3 JUNE

And in every work that he began in the service of the house of God, and in the law, and in the commandments, to seek his God, he did it with all his heart, and prospered.

—2 Chronicles 31:21

God is a kind Father. He sets us all in the places where he wishes us to be employed; and that employment is truly "our Father's business." He chooses work for every creature which will be delightful to them, if they do it simply and humbly. He gives us always strength enough, and sense enough, for what he wants us to do; if we either tire ourselves or puzzle ourselves, it is our own fault. And we may always be sure, whatever we are doing, that we cannot be pleasing him, if we are not happy ourselves.

JOHN RUSKIN (1819–1900)

For further thought:
1. Can I do my daily tasks "in the name of the Lord"?
2. Am I doing anything on a regular basis that I cannot do "with all my heart"?

With all my heart, today I will:

I am the good shepherd, and know my sheep, and am known of mine.
—John 10:14

God knows us through and through. Not the most secret thought, which we must hide from ourselves, is hidden from him. As then we come to know ourselves through and through, we come to see ourselves more as God sees us, and then we catch some little glimpse of his designs with us, how each ordering of his Providence, each check to our desires, each failure of our hopes, is just fitted for us, and for something in our own spiritual state, which, till then, we knew not. Until we come to this knowledge, we must take all in faith, believing, though we know not, the goodness of God towards us. As we know ourselves, we, thus far, know God.

E. B. PUSEY (1800–1882)

For further thought:
1. Am I trying to hide anything from God?
2. If my life is an "open book" to God, should I be equally open with those around me?

Lord, help me to open myself to you and to others. Today I will:

5 JUNE

Let us conduct ourselves becomingly as in the day, not in reveling and drunkenness, not in debauchery and licentiousness, not in quarreling and jealousy.

—Romans 13:13, RSV

Jealousy is in pretty poor company here. It's usually considered one of those "respectable" sins, relegated to a low place on the list of no-nos. But Paul apparently considers it a pretty serious problem, ranking it with some of the most heinous sins in the catalog of evil. St. Chrysostom (A.D. 347?–407), one of the early church fathers, also considered it serious because of its effect on the one who is jealous: "As the moth gnaws a garment, so does envy consume a man." We Christians are not immune to the ravages of jealousy. It's one of the most subtle attacks Satan makes upon us—but it's as destructive and dangerous as a moth let loose in a woolen sweater! But Paul points out the secret of victory over this subtle sin when he says, "Put on the Lord Jesus Christ, and make no provision for the flesh, to gratify its desires" (Rom. 13:14, RSV). Lord, help me with my armor.

For further thought:
1. Am I guilty of jealousy toward someone near to me?
2. Have I experienced jealous feelings in the past? Toward whom?

Today I will place on the altar my jealousy of:

For that person must not suppose that a double-minded man, unstable in all his ways, will receive anything from the Lord.

                                       —James 1:8, RSV

Jesus was talking about this "double-mindedness" when he said, "He who is not with me is against me, and he who does not gather with me scatters" (Matt. 12:30, RSV). He was also referring to the same divided state of mind when he said, "Every kingdom divided against itself is laid waste, and no city or house divided against itself will stand" (Matt. 12:25, RSV). To be double-minded is about as dangerous as driving the wrong way up a one-way street! Such a practice can get you killed! That's true in the spiritual realm, too. "How long halt ye between two opinions?" Elijah asked the Israelites (1 Kings 18:21). That's the question we must all face. We choose for Christ or against him. We proceed with a mind single to his service—or we "halt" with a double mind that hesitates and fails to move forward at all. Lord, help me not to be double-minded!

For further thought:
1. Is there anything in my life right now about which I am "double-minded"?
2. Am I halting between two opinions when I should be moving ahead?

Lord, help me to be single-minded in the Lord's service today as I decide about:

7 JUNE

Read 2 John 4–6

Love does no wrong to a neighbor; therefore love is the fulfilling of the law.

—Romans 13:10, RSV

A heart unloving among kindred has no love toward God's saints and angels. If we have a cold heart toward a servant or a friend, why should we wonder if we have no fervor toward God? If we are cold in our private prayers, we should be earthly and dull in the most devout religious order. If we cannot bear the vexations of a companion, how should we bear the contradiction of sinners? If a little pain overcomes us, how could we endure a cross? If we have no tender, cheerful, affectionate love to those with whom our daily hours are spent, how should we feel the pulse and ardor of love to the unknown and the evil, the ungrateful and repulsive?

H. E. MANNING (1808–1892)

For further thought:
1. In what ways do I show my love to my neighbor?
2. In what ways do I limit my concern for those outside my family circle?
3. To whom should I reach out in love today?

Lord, today I will reach out with your love to:

It is right not to eat meat or drink wine or do anything that makes your brother stumble.

—Romans 14:21, RSV

"Am I my brother's keeper?" is a question as old as man. Cain, Adam's oldest son, spat it out when God questioned him about the whereabouts of his younger brother, Abel (see Gen. 4:9). And it is a question that comes down to our present day with just as strong an impact. How do I answer the question? If I overlook the needs of those less fortunate than I, if I turn away from the pleading eyes of the starving souls in the third world, if one of my actions, public or private, causes a weaker Christian to question his faith, then I must answer Cain's question with a resounding "no." But if I look at life as my Savior did, and feel every need of those around me, remaining sensitive to their cries for help—if I am careful not to cause my weaker brother or sister to stumble—then I am replying a hearty "yes" to Cain's cynical question. Lord, which is it?

For further thought:
1. Have I failed to be "my brother's keeper" in a specific instance recently?
2. What opportunities do I have right now to be my brother's keeper?

Today I will:

For he that is entered into his rest, he also hath ceased from his own works, as God did from his.

—Hebrews 4:10

How shall we rest in God? By giving ourselves wholly to him. If you give yourself by halves, you cannot find full rest; there will ever be a lurking disquiet in that half which is withheld. Martyrs, confessors and saints have tasted this rest, and "counted themselves happy in that they endured." A countless host of God's faithful servants have drunk deeply of it under the daily burden of a weary life—dull, commonplace, painful, or desolate. All that God has been to them he is ready to be to you. The heart once fairly given to God, with a clear conscience, a fitting rule of life, and a steadfast purpose of obedience, you will find a wonderful sense of rest coming over you.

JEAN NICHOLAS GROU (1731–1803)

For further thought:
1. Am I able to "let go and let God"?
2. Is there something in my life right now that hinders me from entering the rest God has for me?

Lord, today I will rest in you by giving you:

Now faith is the substance of things hoped for, the evidence of things not seen.

—Hebrews 11:1

Faith is a fascinating subject. Its true character is rather difficult to pin down. But some rather simple examples and illustrations of faith surround us in everyday life. When I place a letter in the mailbox, I am exhibiting faith of a sort—faith that someone will come along and transport that letter on its way. If I held on to the letter rather than letting it go, I would never get an answer! And every time we drive along a two-lane highway or busy city street, we're exercising faith in the drivers of the oncoming cars—that they are sane, sober, and in control of their vehicles. When we unquestioningly obey a traffic signal we're displaying faith in a man-made traffic-signal system and apparatus. Why then is it sometimes so difficult to have implicit faith in an almighty God who is in control of the universe he created?

For further thought:
1. Where do I most frequently place my faith?
2. Where does my faith seem to break down in practical living?

Lord, today I will have faith to:

11 JUNE

Read 1 Thessalonians 5:12–22

The Lord gave, and the Lord hath taken away; blessed be the name of the Lord.

—Job 1:21

We are ready to praise when all shines fair; but when life is overcast, when all things seem to be against us, when we are in fear for some cherished happiness, or in the depths of sorrow, or in the solitude of a life which has no visible support, or in a season of sickness, and with the shadow of death approaching—then to praise God? Then to say, This fear, loneliness, affliction, pain, and trembling awe are as sure tokens of love as life, health, joy, and the gifts of home? "The Lord gave, and the Lord hath taken away"; on either side it is He, and all is love alike; "blessed be the name of the Lord"—this is the true sacrifice of praise. What can come amiss to a soul which is so in accord with God? What can make so much as one jarring tone in all its harmony? In all the changes of this fitful life, it ever dwells in praise.

H. E. MANNING (1808–1892)

For further thought:
1. Do I tend to cling too closely to the things I love in this world?
2. Can I truly praise God in the midst of testing? How can I learn this attitude of constant praise?

Lord, today I praise you for:

"Do not lay a hand on the boy," he said. "Do not do anything to him. Now I know that you fear God, because you have not withheld from me your son, your only son."

—Genesis 22:12, NIV

At first glance it seems that God was capricious in this whole episode with Abraham and the commanded sacrifice of his son Isaac. At one moment he seemed to be saying to Abraham, "Sacrifice your son to me!" and the next he was saying, "Stop!" Did God really just change his mind here? I don't believe so. He knows the end from the beginning—in his sight a day is as a thousand years, says Peter. God knew that the lesson in obedience he was trying to teach Abraham was needed. It was a test Abraham passed with flying colors even though he didn't even realize he was *being* tested. And there must have been a tremendous lesson here for the young and impressionable Isaac as well. Thank God he is interested in the "training" business—and is patient with me while he is testing me!

For further thought:
1. Is God trying to teach me something right now?
2. Do I have an "Isaac" I need to give to him?

Today I will:

13 JUNE

The Lord knows the days of the blameless, and their heritage will abide for ever; they are not put to shame in evil times, in the days of famine they have abundance.

—Psalm 37:18, 19, RSV

Foundations are important in building homes or roads. There is a widespread "fault" running through the area of Central Texas where I live, and houses built on that fault just don't last. Sooner or later the foundation shifts, and the floor of the house sags or slants steeply in one direction or another. Streets and highways built on the fault suffer a similar fate—they develop strange holes or mysterious "rises," regardless of how carefully they are built. The fault lies in the "fault"! No matter how carefully the foundation is laid, if it is on shifting ground, it will not remain stable and steady. My life is like that. Built on the shifting sand of shallow circumstance, it is bound to break up. Established on the solid foundation of Jesus Christ, however, it will withstand whatever comes. "Their heritage will abide for ever."

For further thought:
1. Are there any "shaky foundations" in my life?
2. Is my life lived "above" or "below" circumstances?

Because my "heritage" is assured, today I will:

God is our refuge and strength, a very present help in trouble.
Therefore will not we fear, though the earth be removed, and though
the mountains be carried into the midst of the sea.

—Psalm 46:1, 2

Our external circumstances may change. Toil may take the place
of rest, sickness of health, trials may thicken within and without.
Externally, we are the prey of such circumstances; but if our heart
is stayed on God, no changes or chances can touch it, and all that
may befall us will but draw us closer to him. Whatever the present
moment may bring, our knowledge that it is his will, and that our
future heavenly life will be influenced by it, will make all not only
tolerable, but welcome to us, while no vicissitudes can affect us
greatly, knowing that he who holds us in his powerful hand cannot
change, but abides forever.

JEAN NICHOLAS GROU (1731–1803)

For further thought:
1. Am I able to remain serene in the midst of my pressures?
2. What does it mean to "anchor my soul" on God?

Today I will:

15 JUNE

Now therefore, I pray thee, if I have found favor in thy sight, show me now thy ways, that I may know thee and find favor in thy sight. Consider too that this nation is thy people.

—Exodus 33:13

God gives us direction that is clear-cut and specific. He promises us, as he did Moses, "My presence will go with you, and I will give you rest" (v. 14). He leads his children today just as specifically and definitely as he led his people out of Egypt. How does this work? I've found that if I'm reading the Scriptures, if I'm in fellowship with other Christians, if my prayer life is up-to-date—all these factors enter into giving me guidance. God can speak to me through his people and his Word to show me his will. Sometimes circumstances indicate God's direction for me, too. When he closes a door, it's the height of foolishness for me to force my way through—even though I sometimes do it!

For further thought:
1. Is God showing me a particular "way" today?
2. How has God spoken to me most recently?

Lord, I ask specific guidance to:

JUNE 16

Be ye therefore merciful, as your Father also is merciful.

—Luke 6:36

It is related about a great artist that he was once wandering in the mountains of Switzerland when the police met him and demanded his passport. "I do not have it with me," he replied, "but my name is Dore." "Prove it, if you are," replied the officers, knowing who Dore was, but not believing that this was he. Taking a piece of paper, the artist hastily sketched a group of peasants who were standing near, and did it with such grace and skill that the officials exclaimed, "Enough! You are Dore."

The world cares little for a mere profession. We say we are Christians, but the challenge is, "Prove it." If we are of Christ we must be able to do the work of Christ, to live the life of Christ, to show the spirit of Christ. The artist's skilful drawing proved his identity. We must prove that we are the followers of our Master by the love, the grace, the beauty, the holiness of our life.

J. R. MILLER (1840–1912)

For further thought:
1. If I had to prove I was a Christian, what would I do?
2. Should my witness be passive—just "living the life"—or could I show my faith in other ways more effectively?

To "prove" my faith, today I will:

If ye, then, being evil, know how to give good gifts unto your children, how much more shall your heavenly Father give the Holy Spirit to them that ask him?

—Luke 11:13

No true, faith-winged prayer goes unanswered, but many a prayer that seems to us unanswered is really *overanswered*. God does not grant the actual thing we ask, because he is able to do something infinitely better for us. We ask only for bodily help or relief, and he sees that we have more need for some deep spiritual blessing. He answers our soul's needs before he gratifies our personal wishes. We ask for a temporal favor; he does not give it to us, but instead he gives us a spiritual good which will enrich us forever. We ask for the removal of a burden or the avoiding of a sorrow; our plea is not granted in form, but instead we receive a new impartation of the power of Christ, or an angel comes from heaven and ministers to us. Thus many times our little prayers are really overanswered.

For further thought:
1. Have I had an "overanswered" prayer recently?
2. Do I tend to "underask" in my prayer life?

Today I will:

Let love be without dissimulation. Abhor that which is evil; cleave to that which is good.

—Romans 12:9

It is impossible for us to make the duties of our lot minister to our sanctification without a habit of devout fellowship with God. This is the spring of all our life, and the strength of it. It is prayer, meditation, and converse with God that refreshes, restores, and renews the temper of our minds, at all times, under all trials, after all conflicts with the world. By this contact with the world unseen we receive continual accesses of strength. As our day, so is our strength. Without this healing and refreshing of spirit, duties grow to be burdens, the events of life chafe our temper, employments lower the tone of our minds, and we become fretful, irritable, and impatient.

H. E. MANNING (1808–1892)

For further thought:
1. Is my prayer life "real" enough to help me grow?
2. Am I depending daily on the strength God alone can give?

Lord, today I ask specifically that you will help me:

Therefore I tell you, do not be anxious about your life, what you shall eat or what you shall drink, nor about your body, what you shall put on. Is not life more than food, and the body more than clothing?
—Matthew 6:25, RSV

Jesus practiced what he preached! In spite of the pressures upon him, he moved serenely through hectic days and busy nights, seemingly untouched by the chaos and confusion around him. There is no question about it—our lives in this modern, fast-moving world are subjected to pressures perhaps unlike any Jesus faced. As Alvin Toffler points out so graphically in his book, *Future Shock,* our rapid, pell-mell pace may be leading us to destruction. But I am convinced that Jesus would have moved as serenely through this world as he did the New Testament milieu. And he wants us to be as serene in the midst of the duties and uncertainties that surround us. He, busier and more burdened than we, would have us enjoy the inner poise and peace that come from total dependence upon and confidence in him. Through that relationship of trust we can overcome an alien world which seeks our ruin. As Jesus did, we can live one day at a time!

For further thought:
1. What was Jesus' secret of serenity?
2. Is the same source of power available to me?

Living "one day at a time," today I will:

Thus will I bless thee while I live: I will lift up my hands in thy name.
—Psalm 63:4

Many of David's psalms, this among them, are really prayers. In this and other instances David shows an insight into prayer that many of us modern Christians completely miss: We are so prone to ask God for gifts or *things* in our prayers, but too often we fail to recognize that the greatest and most satisfying gift of all is the Giver himself! Even though we are unaware of our real and deepest desire—companionship with the heavenly Father—God knows our need and offers himself freely to us. This is the spirit in which David prayed here in Psalm 63—an awareness of the presence of the living God. David was hiding out in the Judean desert, but his companion was the living and eternal God!

For further thought:
1. Are my prayers full of praise—or petitions?
2. Am I living to "bless" God?

Lord, today I praise you for:

But he listened! He heard my prayer! He paid attention to it. Blessed be God who didn't turn away when I was praying, and didn't refuse me his kindness and love.

—Psalm 66:19, 20, LB

Prayer is a vast subject—its meaning cannot be probed in a moment of time. But the psalmist's prayer here *does* suggest three aspects of prayer of which I need to be reminded almost daily, for I forget them so soon. First, prayer is really conversation with God, in which he both *hears* what I say and *responds* to me—perhaps not verbally, but graciously and lovingly. Second, prayer is a personal privilege in which I should take great delight. With the psalmist I should shout: "... he listened! He heard my prayer! He paid attention to it!" And third, faithful, consistent, *daily* prayer opens my life to God's power. What a thrill to know that the "secret" of power is not secret at all. It's simply being *connected* to the Source of power. Lord, let me walk close to you as the psalmist did.

For further thought:
1. I know God listens to me, but do I listen to him?
2. Do I take my prayer privilege for granted—or do I grasp the greatness of my opportunity and treat it accordingly?

Because God hears me, today I will:

If you sit down, you will not be afraid; when you lie down, your sleep will be sweet.

—Proverbs 3:24, RSV

To most, sleep is a pretty mundane subject—prosaic and dull, to say the least. But Solomon in the Psalms and Proverbs elevated it to a place of greater importance—indeed, in his eyes it is a gracious gift from God. Nature uses no halfway measures. For each need there is a satisfaction. For the eye there is light, for the ear there is sound, for the wing there is air, and for the tired body there is the darkness and quiet of the night. To primitive people the black mystery of the dark is frightening. To children overwhelmed by scary tales of terror, it is still frightening. But to those of us who have happy and confident spirits, it is the space in which "God giveth his beloved sleep." For the solemn hush and gentle calm of the night we must be ever grateful.

For further thought:
1. Do I appreciate the blessing of restful sleep?
2. If not, is there something in my life that hinders my relationship with others and my communion with God—and causes me unrest?

As I go to my rest tonight, I will:

The day is thine, the night also is thine: thou hast prepared the light and the sun.

—Psalm 74:16

This passage from the Psalms pretty well sums up the creation story. It reminds me of God's words in Genesis 1: "And God said, Let there be lights in the firmament of the heaven to divide the day from the night; and let them be for signs and for seasons and for days and years: and let them be for lights in the firmament of the heaven to give light upon the earth, and it was so" (vv. 14, 15). I am one of God's "lesser lights" in the sense that I *reflect* his greater light. The source of my light comes from him and not from myself—and this is good news. But the fashion in which it is reflected is peculiarly my own and has its place in the firmament of God's earthly family. I am a unique person, and not a duplication or mimeographed copy of anyone else. I have my own sphere of influence and "comfort zone" where I operate, and I am responsible to share my faith in a way that fits my personality and lifestyle. Am I doing so as one who was "established" (RSV) by him?

For further thought:
1. To whom can I most effectively minister?
2. Am I doing anything to reach out to those I encounter in my daily life?
3. Does ministering to those in my immediate "sphere of influence" relieve me of responsibility to reach those outside of it?

As a "reflector" of God's light, today I will:

And out of the ground made the Lord God to grow every tree that is
pleasant to the sight, and good for food; the tree of life also in the
midst of the garden, and the tree of knowledge of good and evil.
—Genesis 2:9

The song says, "God is so wonderful"—and he truly is! He could
have made black, ugly fruit and garishly colorful trees, but instead
he made beautiful red apples and green trees, restful to the eye,
with shapes symmetrical and pleasing to the viewer. Truly he united beauty and utility in a masterful display of skill. Not only is the
fruit he designed beautiful to look upon, but it meets many of my
nutritional needs. What God supplies is good as well as beautiful. It
is only as man has stepped into the picture and destroyed the
"balance of nature," as it were, that complications have arisen and
imbalance has occurred. How thankful I am that God can take my
life and make something beautiful of it so long as I submit to him
and do not try to "improve" upon his workmanship.

For further thought:
1. What is going on in my life right now that is "utilitarian"
   as well as beautiful?
2. Just because something is practical, do I view it as less
   than beautiful?

Lord, take hold of my life today and:

25 JUNE

In the Lord do I take refuge.

—Psalm 11:1

The writer of this psalm illustrated in his life what it means to have faith. Faith is a complex and many-faceted thing. It is impossible to define to the satisfaction of every person, but illustrations and examples abound in the Scriptures and in life. One of the greatest men of faith, George Mueller, said of this facet of the Christian life: "The only way to learn strong faith is to endure great trials. I have learned my faith by standing firm amid severe testing."

In one sense of the word, faith *is* learned. There are those who would question this statement, but there are illustrations from life to back it up. Those who win Olympic medals are more than just gifted athletes. They are dedicated, disciplined, and devoted to their sport or specialty. An Olympic athlete may devote as many as ten or twelve years to training for his or her particular event. Weather, all kinds of obstacles, or disappointments do not keep him or her from training, preparing for victory. In the spiritual realm, too, it takes dedication, discipline, and devotion to develop great faith.

For further thought:
1. Am I in training in the school of faith?
2. When is the last time I consciously took "refuge" in the Lord?

To "build" my faith, today I will:

"Of course we may eat it," the woman told him. "It's only the fruit from the tree at the center of the garden that we are not to eat. God says we mustn't eat it or even touch it, or we will die."

—Genesis 3:3, LB

Someone has said, "Never put a question mark where God has placed a period." In essence, that is what Eve did when she fell for Satan's scheme to plant the tiny, seemingly harmless seed of doubt in her mind. His "has God said?" comes to us in various guises today. Temptations to disobey God's clear-cut commands or the dictates of conscience touch all of us. A tendency to "doubt at night what God has told us in the day" plagues most of God's people at one time or another. I wonder if we really believe God's unequivocable tone in this portion of Scripture?

For further thought:
1. If I really believed God means what he says, what would I do differently today?
2. Has Satan put one over on me lately?

The next time I am tempted to doubt God, I will:

27 JUNE

Lord, thou hast been our dwelling place in all generations.
—Psalm 90:1

In our chaotic and confused world, not many things remain unchanged. Down through the changing years of our lives, however, there has been one constant—and that unchanging center is God himself. Nature and history are transformed by change and decay. Our lives, too, are marked by constant change. Of that we can be equally sure. But God does not change! He is ever the same. His will for us remains fixed and abiding, despite our ups and downs, our frequent falls, our occasional wanderings. Despite our lack of stability he remains faithful and steadfast. As Moses says in Psalm 90, he has "been our dwelling place [our home or refuge] in all generations." It is his presence that leads and sustains us—even though we sometimes depart from the way he has established for us.

For further thought:
1. What does the phrase, "in all generations" suggest so far as length of time is concerned?
2. What picture does "dwelling place" or "home" conjure up in my mind?

In the light of God's promises to me, today I will:

Why art thou cast down, O my soul? And why art thou disquieted in me? hope thou in God: for I shall yet praise him for the help of his countenance.

—Psalm 42:5

Over and over again the Bible makes it clear that great souls are built by adversity and difficulty. Grief can be the foundation of stronger faith. Twice in this Psalm (vv. 5 and 11) we are told to "hope in God." When we are called upon to endure difficult circumstances, we should not think of them as sent upon us from the hand of an angry God. Rather, we should let difficult circumstances serve as stepping stones upward to a closer relationship with a loving God. Romans 8:28 tells us that God can use adverse circumstances to work for our good if our lives are committed to him. His gracious purposes for us can be worked out through troubles and disappointments as well as through achievements and joys. Character can grow better in the garden of affliction than in the pond of pleasure.

For further thought:
1. Do I have a relationship with God as strong and enduring as that of the psalmist?
2. What does the psalmist mean when he says "hope in God"?

In light of what I have learned in this psalm, I will:

Buy the truth, and sell it not; also wisdom, and instruction, and understanding.

—Proverbs 23:23

The wise man is here talking about letting my Christian commitment permeate all of my life. On this very subject, J. R. Miller has this to say: "One of the most harmful practical errors of common Christian living is the cutting of life into two sections—a religious and a secular section. We acknowledge God in the religious part. We fence off days and little spaces of time in each day which we profess to give to worship, devotion. But the danger is that we confine our acknowledging of God to these set times and seasons, while we shut him out of our real life. That is not true religion which prays well, and soars away into celestial raptures and holy dreams while it has no effect on one's daily common life down here in the paths of toil and duty. We should have our visions, but we must bring them down into our earthly experience and make them real there."

For further thought:
1. Am I trying to apply my Christian commitment to all of my life—or am I guilty of "layering," dividing my life into secular and sacred areas?
2. When is the last time I put a "dream" into practice?

Today I will:

You have made wide steps beneath my feet so that I need never slip.
—Psalm 18:36, LB

Do we take the blessings that the common days bring to us? Do we extract the honey from every flower that grows by our path? Do not angels come to us unawares in homely or unattractive disguise, walk with us, talk with us, and then only become known to us when they have flown away—when their places are empty? Shall we not learn to see the goodness and the beauty in the gifts that God sends to us? Their very commonness veils their blessedness. Let us seek for the good in everything. Then, though we see it not, let us never doubt that it lies hidden in every gift of God to us. Every moment brings us some benediction. Even the rough hand of trial holds in its clasp for us some treasure of love.

J. R. MILLER (1840–1912)

For further consideration:

1. What are some of the "wide places" I can identify in my life?
2. Do I sometimes miss "the wideness of God's mercy" because it is so available to me?

In recognition of the "wideness" available to me, today I will:

1 JULY

And Jesus went with him....

—Mark 5:24

What a world of truth is wrapped up in these few short words. Jairus was swamped with fear for his daughter's life, but when he came into the presence of Jesus, he was filled with faith. Then come the beautiful words, "Jesus went with him." As Jairus started back to his daughter's bedside, Jesus was beside him. This much you can count on—whether it's to a sickbed, or into circumstances that wound and wither the soul, the Lord goes with his own. No matter what the difficulties, not only does he go *with* me—he has been there before me! I'm surrounded by his care, and nothing really harmful can happen to me there!

For further thought:

1. Into what circumstances do I want Jesus to go with me today?
2. How can I open myself to his care?

Today I will:

He [the Lord] spoke to them in the pillar of cloud.

—Psalm 99:7, RSV

Moses and Aaron are not the only ones to whom the Lord has spoken. By his Word and his Spirit he speaks to each of his children today. If we are believers, his words take one of two tacks: they are either commendatory or critical. Either they encourage us or they warn us. Strangely, we are often so busy pursuing our personal goals that we do not hear either kind of words. We need to quiet our hearts so that we can hear him—whether he speaks in a cloud or in a still, small voice.

For further thought:
1. What has the Lord said to me today?
2. Have I delved into the Word for his message today?

Today I will:

3 JULY

... Work hard and with gladness all the time, as though working for Christ, doing the will of God with all your heart.
—Ephesians 6:7, LB

Is it possible to face the tasks of the day with a positive point of view? Can we follow Paul's admonition in Colossians 3:23: "Whatsoever ye do, do it heartily, as to the Lord, and not unto men"? It *is* possible to sacramentalize our daily routine. I can hang this verse over the kitchen sink, the work bench, or the desk—and discover the difference attitude can make toward the daily tasks that can so easily become drudgery. If we make Jesus our boss—instead of the sink, bench, or desk—we will discover that the routine can become rich in texture as we seek to glorify him, no matter how mundane the task.

For further thought:
1. Am I involved in the kind of work that can be done "unto the Lord"?
2. Am I doing my work in this spirit?
3. If not, why not?

To accomplish my tasks "as unto the Lord" today I will:

The light of the body is the eye: therefore, when thine eye is single, thy whole body is also full of light.

—Luke 11:34

The thought Jesus is conveying here is the simplicity of the mind's eye. Having a "single eye" means having clearness of vision, without any foreign matter obliterating the image the eye receives. It means accuracy of vision—not seeing double or distorted images, but seeing each object exactly as it is. Having a "single eye" also means having concentration of vision, focusing on one all-important object—or Person! When we have such a singleness in our mind's eye, we are filled with light—our conscience is clear, our heart is at rest, and faith can function freely. When that singleness is disturbed—for instance, when we try to serve both God and mammon—we deceive ourselves, and a darkness comes over the soul.

There is nothing more necessary in our walk with God than that we should look with a "single eye" on only one supreme object of love—God. I must strive for singleness of aim and simplicity of purpose, and then I will know what it is to walk in the "light of life" (see meditation for July 5).

For further thought:
1. Does this passage describe the state of my soul?
2. Is this kind of life—lived with singleness of vision—really possible?
3. Is there any "double vision" distorting my life now?

Lord, help me look with a "single eye" today as I:

5 JULY

And Jesus said unto him, No man, having put his hand to the plough, and looking back, is fit for the kingdom of God.
—Luke 9:62

The Christian life should be marked by definiteness, simplicity of aim, and steady endurance. This was stressed in yesterday's meditation, which looked at the importance of focusing with a "single eye" on God and his kingdom. Today's scripture deals with "ploughing straight ahead" in singleness of purpose, resisting anything that would distract us from our task.

But is this singlemindedness possible without neglecting earthly duties? Can I give myself to do one thing wholly without neglecting many temporal matters? Look at a ship on the way to some distant port. One main purpose controls all her movements: to reach her destination in safety. There is a good deal of activity on board. Many duties have to be done daily, calling for careful diligence and prompt obedience. But there is one thing being done constantly, and in this all aboard are concerned—pressing toward the mark, the port. So it is with life's great aim in pursuing the Christian course. To accomplish God's plan for me, I need to make the primary purpose of my life to be involved in his ongoing kingdom (see meditation for July 4).

For further thought:
1. Where are my priorities being placed—on temporal matters or eternal concerns?
2. What is my concept of the "kingdom of God"?

With God's kingdom as my ongoing purpose, today I will:

All that believed were together, and had all things common.
　　　　　　　　　　　　　　　　　　—Acts 2:44

The J. B. Phillips translation says, "All the believers shared everything in common; they sold their possessions and goods and divided the proceeds among the fellowship according to individual need." This kind of love and fellowship is not, I'm afraid, typical of most Christian groups today. Rather, we seem to bring into the fellowship of believers the same suspicions, jealousies, and frictions common in the world around us. I wonder what would happen if we modern Christians would really love each other as those early believers did. I think then the description in verse 47, "And the Lord added to the church daily such as should be saved," would be true of the church today, just as it was of the early church.

For further reflection:
1. What am I doing to encourage this kind of a loving atmosphere in my church?
2. Do I, personally, live out this kind of a commitment?

Today I will:

7 JULY

Read Luke 6:27–38

Give, and it will be given to you; good measure, pressed down, shaken together, running over, will be put into your lap. For the measure you give will be the measure you get back.
—Luke 6:38, RSV

The lifestyle Jesus is calling for here might be summed up in the phrase, "Give more than you expect to get." This is a philosophy foreign to our "success"-oriented society—but in God's economy, it works extremely well. If I give of myself to those around me—my family, business associates, fellow church members, and so on—God will use his measure to give back to me. And, try as I will, I cannot outgive God. If I give out love, I will receive even more love in return—perhaps not from the person I gave it to, but in some other way. God is the Master Mathematician, and his measure, "pressed down, shaken together, running over, will be put into your lap." If I love liberally, I will be loved liberally in return.

For further reflection:
1. Am I "stingy" in giving of myself?
2. Do I give with the motivation to get in return?

Lord, let me give myself today to:

But the more the Egyptians mistreated and oppressed them, the more the Israelis seemed to multiply! The Egyptians became alarmed.
—Exodus 1:12, LB

There is a stirring spiritual principle at work here that I need to remember. In the Christian life, oppression and adversity or affliction result in greater fruitfulness. Just as the Israelites multiplied under mistreatment, so Christians produce better and more lasting fruit when they are pressed by adversity. It is a fact of physics that water becomes steam when it is heated. Steam is a tremendously powerful force, much more so than the water from which it comes. In the same way, the true Christian under pressure becomes more powerful in his effectiveness as a Christian. Persecution produces patience and the other fruits of the Spirit, which in turn allow the Christian to make a greater impact on his world.

For further thought:
1. What effect has persecution had on my life?
2. Am I growing under pressure, or am I giving in to it?

Lord, help me become more fruitful when under adversity. Today I will:

9 JULY

God hath caused me to be fruitful in the land of my affliction.
—Genesis 41:52

These were Joseph's words in reference to his second-born son, Ephraim. Joseph's true home, after all, was in Canaan; Egypt was "the land of his affliction." But even there God had made Joseph fruitful and blessed him. He was thankful for the past—even with all its sorrow.

So the believer today may often look back upon times of bitter trial and see how God has made them times of special fruitfulness. Not that affliction necessarily sanctifies the heart or causes us to glorify God. After all, the secret of our spiritual progress does not lie in our circumstances. None can sanctify our souls or cause us to be fruitful but the Triune God. But he often uses our adversities to humble our hearts, subdue our pride, and make us submissive. Then it is that he causes us to be fruitful in the land of our affliction. "From me comes your fruit" says the Lord through the prophet Hosea (14:8, RSV). God is the only source of our fruitfulness as Christians.

For further thought:
1. What is my usual attitude under trial or "affliction"?
2. What or whom has God used recently to "humble" me?

My lesson from affliction today is:

And Ruth said, Entreat me not to leave thee, or to return from following after thee: for whither thou goest, I will go; and where thou lodgest I will lodge: thy people shall be my people, thy God my God.

—Ruth 1:16

Confronted with a crisis situation, Ruth made a deliberate choice—to follow Naomi's God. She could not remain loyal to Naomi without doing so. On the subject of choice for life, G. Campbell Morgan (1863–1945) says; "Density is fixed by the choice of the human will, which selects for itself its heaven or hell. Thus each one of us is building character forever. Those who are yielding to the forces around that mar the life do so absolutely of their own free choice." Ruth chose for God, and the experience of the rest of her life bore out the wisdom of that choice. With Joshua she could say, "Choose you this day whom you will serve . . . but as for me and my house, we will serve the Lord" (Josh. 24:15). May my choice be the same!

For further thought:
1. Is my role in life the result of my choice?
2. Have I chosen to "yield to" or resist the forces around me that "mar" my life?

Lord, help me to choose wisely in accordance with your will today as I:

11 JULY

That no one be immoral or irreligious like Esau, who sold his birthright for a single meal. For you know that afterward, when he desired to inherit the blessing, he was rejected, for he found no chance to repent, though he sought it with tears.

—Hebrews 12:16, 17, RSV

Esau's experience summarized here teaches us a vitally important lesson: Sometimes "spur-of-the-moment" decisions determine our destiny. All because he let his momentary physical hunger dominate his life, Esau gave up his priceless spiritual heritage. He passed up eternal blessings for the sake of temporary satisfaction. He sacrificed on the altar of the immediate what God had promised him for eternity. Though he repented at leisure, the decision he had made on the spur of the moment could not be undone. If it could happen to Esau, it could happen to me.

For further thought:
1. Have I ever sacrificed a long-term good on the altar of the immediate?
2. What needs or "hungers" are strong enough to cause me to compromise eternal values?

Because I've learned a lesson from Esau, today I will:

And it came to pass, when God destroyed the cities of the plain, that God remembered Abraham and sent Lot out of the midst of the overthrow, when he overthrew the cities in which Lot dwelt.

—Genesis 19:29

What a striking contrast there is between Lot and Abraham, despite the fact that both had the same opportunity to walk with God. The difference was that Lot chose selfishly (Gen. 13) and "pitched... towards Sodom" whereas Abraham chose wisely and "built... an altar to the Lord" (Gen. 13:18) wherever he went. As we look at Lot we see one whom the world would call a winner—a shrewd businessman alert to every opportunity to "make it." He chose what seemed the best land and the most sagacious society, while Abraham took what seemed "second best." But on God's scale Abraham made the higher choice—to follow the Father's will—while Lot chose the limited horizon of selfishness and self-will.

For further thought:
1. Which choice have I made?
2. If I'm looking like Lot is it too late to change?

Lord, today I have the chance to choose either selfishly or wisely. I choose to:

Behold, I have done according to thy words: lo, I have given thee a wise and understanding heart; so that there was none like thee before thee, neither after thee shall any arise like unto thee.

—1 Kings 3:12

Solomon here exemplifies a trait every Christian wishes he had—common sense, or what some would call "instinctive insight." Daniel had it as well (see Dan. 1), and differed from Solomon in that, so far as we know, he never lost it. He went to his reward "a wise old man" while Solomon in his later years declined in wisdom and influence in his world. Indeed, by the time of his death he had so declined that he had virtually lost the kingdom his father David had so laboriously built up. Lord, may I be like Daniel and not like Solomon!

For further thought:

1. In what ways do Solomon and Daniel seem similar?
2. In what ways do they differ?
3. What can I personally learn from them?

To follow Daniel's example, today I will:

The Lord giveth wisdom; out of his mouth cometh knowledge and understanding.

—Proverbs 2:6

How often in our daily walk do we find ourselves in need of wisdom? Wisdom, according to James, is one of those gifts which God has promised to bestow upon us: "If any of you lack wisdom, let him ask of God, that giveth to all men liberally, and upbraideth not; and it shall be given him" (James 1:5). But there is more to it than that! We read: "But of him are ye in Christ Jesus, who of God is made unto us wisdom" (1 Cor. 1:30). Here, then, we learn wisdom is not so much a gift we are to seek apart from Christ, but that which we may expect to find *in* him. He is our Wisdom as truly as he is our Righteousness and our Strength. Our weakness is the sphere in which his strength finds its fullest fruition; he is ready and willing to fill our emptiness with his own grace and fullness. There is need for a daily hearing of his voice—a continual reception of his Word. For it is not our natural reasoning powers that will guide us correctly, or give us right judgment in all things. No, Christ alone is our Wisdom.

For further thought:
1. Does it feel natural for me to look to the Lord for wisdom?
2. How practical is this wisdom of which the Bible speaks?

Lord, today I need your wisdom as I:

And he was sad at that saying, and went away grieved: for he had great possessions.

—Mark 10:22

This young man had a money problem most of us don't have—too much! But Jesus was talking more about attitude here than he was about wealth. J. H. Jowett puts it in perspective for us: "Dr. F. B. Meyer has told us how his early Christian life was marred and his ministry paralyzed just because he had kept back one key from the bunch of keys to his heart which he had given the Lord. Every key save one! The key of one room of his heart was kept for personal use, and the Lord was shut out. And the effects of this incomplete consecration were found in lack of power, lack of assurance, lack of joy and peace. The 'joy of the Lord' begins when we hand over the last key. We sit with Christ on his throne as soon as we have surrendered all our crowns and made him sole and only ruler of our life and its possessions."

For further thought:
1. What "room" in my heart am I reserving for self?
2. Once I turn over a key to the Lord, is it possible for me to take it back again?

Lord, with you in complete charge of my life, today I will:

Simon Peter, a servant and an apostle of Jesus Christ, to them that have obtained like precious faith with us through the righteousness of God and our Savior Jesus Christ: Grace and peace be multiplied unto you through the knowledge of God, and of Jesus our Lord.

—2 Peter 1:1, 2

Martin Luther (1483–1546), the great reformer, said of this verse: "These two words, *grace* and *peace*, contain in them the whole sum of Christianity. Grace contains the remission of sins; peace, a quiet and joyful conscience. When the grace and peace of God are in the heart, then is man strong. Then he can neither be cast down by adversity nor puffed up by prosperity, but walks on evenly, keeping to the highway. It is in the spirit that you find the paradise of grace and peace."

This is the kind of life the apostle Peter sought for Christians in the early church—and the kind of life you and I should enjoy today. Grace and peace are gifts from God that come to us because of our standing in Christ. Because we have been sprinkled with his blood (1 Pet. 1:2) we are assured that we have been justified, cleansed from all sin, and accepted into his heavenly kingdom. With such assurance of his grace, how can we help but have peace?

For further thought:
1. Am I living in this grace and peace of which Peter writes?
2. If not, why not?
3. If so, am I "growing in grace"?

Lord, today help me to grow in grace as I:

17 JULY

Through the tender mercy of our God; whereby the dayspring from on high hath visited us, to give light to them that sit in darkness and in the shadow of death, to guide our feet into the way of peace.
—Luke 1:78, 79

This passage of scripture is called the Song of Zacharias or the "Benedictus." Filled with quotations from the Old Testament, it forecasts the life and ministry of the Lord Jesus. In the midst of everything he encountered and endured, Jesus had a deep, inner peace which sometimes mystified those among whom he walked. Amid the tensions and anxieties of life, it is possible for us to move in quiet confidence and calm—if we know Christ's secret. In him we are freed from the tyranny of circumstances and the shadows of our adverse environment. He teaches us that it is not outward success alone that gives life worth. Our characters grow better in adversity than they do in prosperity. Through Christ we find an inner peace the world cannot give—or take away.

For further thought:
1. What kind of a day do I usually have—pressured or peaceful?
2. What could I do to improve matters?

With the peace that God gives, today I will:

Keep on sowing your seed, for you never know which will grow—perhaps it all will.

—Ecclesiastes 11:6, LB

It seems that for many of us seed-sowing is a forgotten art—but the truth of this proverb is much broader than the farm from which it springs. It is a profound principle of life. In all our contacts with others we are "sowers." Our personalities "rub off" on all those with whom we come in contact. In a way, we carry our bag of seeds through life—and we are forever flinging them into the waiting soil of others' lives. The sowing is inevitable. We scatter seed wherever we go—whether we are conscious of it or not. Our influence is either good or bad, depending upon the life from which it springs.

For further thought:
1. What impact am I having upon those around me?
2. As I look back upon my life, in what direction do I seem to be moving?

Help me, Lord, not to be careless in my sowing. Today I will:

19 JULY

O Lord, how manifold are thy works! In wisdom hast thou made them all; the earth is full of thy riches.

—Psalm 104:24

I have found that a "walk in the woods"—time spent "communing with nature"—can sometimes renew and refresh my spirits more than any other activity. Our lives, especially if we are urban dwellers, become so hurried, harried, and fretful that it does us good to get back to our roots. These lie in nature, in the unsullied solitude, if only we can take time out to soak it in. Ann Landers often tells people to "wake up and smell the coffee." In a sense, that's what the psalmist is telling us here. Such communion with nature will wash our souls with a sense of what the divine Artist through the work of his hands has done. The power and silence of a deep pine forest, or the vast panorama of sea and mountain, can heal our hurting souls and bring balm to the wounds of our worried and baffled lives.

For further reflection:
1. When was the last time I allowed myself time to let God heal my harried soul?
2. What could I do on a daily basis to let God's healing take place?

In search of God's healing touch, today I will:

... lo, I am with you alway, even unto the end of the world. Amen.
—Matthew 28:20

As we look at our circumstances, it is easy to fall into the misconception that Christ has left the world. Looking at the chaos around us, we might easily begin to feel that the only answer to the world's drastic need is for the Lord Jesus to return in spectacular fashion—so that righteousness can once again prevail upon the earth. This he promised his disciples in Matthew 24:30: "they will see the Son of man coming on the clouds of heaven with power and great glory." But we sometimes forget that he also promised his unending presence with us when he said, "Lo, I am with you alway...." He doesn't stay propped up in distant heaven, waiting for a suitable moment to revisit his people. In the blessed Holy Spirit, he is with us *right now* in the midst of our day's work, our personal experiences, and in the all-consuming cause of bringing the entire world to the feet of the Savior—the One who has the answers to life's enigmas.

For further thought:
1. Do I live as if Jesus was "in" my life right now?
2. Is the Holy Spirit real to me?

In the light of God's presence in my life, today I will:

And Caleb stilled the people before Moses, and said, Let us go up at once, and possess it; for we are well able to overcome it. But the men that went up with him said, We be not able to go up against the people; for they are stronger than we.

—Numbers 13:30, 31

Caleb and the other spies saw the same things—a good land peopled by giants. But the other spies saw God in the shadow of the circumstances, while Caleb looked at the circumstances in the shadow of God. Caleb believed God could and would give Israel the victory, despite the fact that they were outnumbered and tiny in stature compared to the giants of the land. The other spies were ready to quit before they started—simply because the giants were more real to them than God was. On which side would I stand? With courageous Caleb, confident in God—or with the cowardly spies, ready to give up without a fight?

For further thought:
1. How do I handle the daily battles that I face—as if God were in charge, or man?
2. If I face overwhelming circumstances, do I see God in the shadow of the circumstances—or the circumstances in the shadow of God?

As I enter my "land of Canaan," today I will:

I call to remembrance my song in the night: I commune with mine own heart: and my spirit made diligent search.

—Psalm 77:6

The Living Bible renders this verse: "Then my nights were filled with joyous songs. I search my soul and meditate upon the difference now." Here's a spiritual lesson I need to remember. If the Lord had not made the night, I would not have had a song. When I look at my circumstances from the underside, I often fail to see their true shape. But when I let God change my perspective and "show me the end from the beginning," everything changes. As the Psalmist says in Psalm 42:8, "By day the Lord commands his steadfast love; and at night his song is with me, a prayer to the God of my life" (RSV). When God allows my faith to be stretched, he's not punishing me—he's giving me a chance to grow!

For further thought:
1. What experiences have "stretched" me lately?
2. Would I rather be insulated from these events?

In the light of your plan for me, O Lord, today I will:

23 JULY

Woe to those who call evil good and good evil, who put darkness for light and light for darkness, who put bitter for sweet and sweet for bitter!

—Isaiah 5:20, RSV

Our perspective determines our destiny. Our failure to see things in their proper proportion places our very lives in peril. It is not necessary that we openly desire to pervert truth—our moral blindness can accomplish that purpose without our willful participation in the process. We blunder into error by our failure to put the facts of life in their correct order. We need the divine perspective if we are going to avoid delusions and self-deception. Knowing the power of untruth to ruin character, to blight happiness, and to sow discord in the world around us, we need to arm ourselves against it by aligning ourselves with the Savior. After all, he is *the* Truth, the Way, and the Life!

For further thought:
1. Am I being deluded in any area of my life by untruth perceived as truth?
2. Is there someone in my life to point this out to me?

Open my eyes, that I may see, Lord, those areas in my life that need change. Today I will:

No longer do I call you servants... but I have called you friends.
—John 15:15, RSV

Great friendships are possible only to great souls. Most of us have business associates, casual acquaintances, and occasional companions. Real friends, on the other hand, are not so easy to acquire. Friendship rests upon more than accidental relationships or even association in a common task. Its roots lie in the spiritual realm. Friends must meet each other at the deeper levels of living. Only an infinity rooted in common ideas and outlook can survive the inevitable misunderstandings and petty frustrations that are a part of the fabric of everyday existence. Robert South (1634–1716), put it this way: "A true friend is the gift of God, and he only who made hearts can unite them."

For further reflection:
1. Who are my real friends?
2. To whom am I a real friend?

In the name of friendship today I will:

See that none of you repays evil for evil, but always seek to do good to one another and to all.

—1 Thessalonians 5:15, RSV

The practical admonition in this passage underlines a life principle: true happiness can be found only in a sincere desire and concern for the happiness of others. Someone has said that those who are wrapped up in themselves make pretty small packages. It's easy to become discontented by nursing the foolish delusion that there is not enough happiness in the world to go around, so you should grab all the gusto you can for yourself this time around—even at the expense of your neighbor's happiness, apparently! This is the path to a constricted corridor of living—a narrowness of vision that shuts out concern for others. Underlying our enduring satisfaction and joy there must be a large and genuine wish for the welfare of others. By this good will our own happiness is enriched, for in the happiness of others our own souls will then have their share of happiness.

For further reflection:
1. Who is most important to me—myself or others?
2. How can I overcome my tendency toward self-centeredness?

Looking toward the welfare of others, Lord, today I will:

He came to his own home, and his own people received him not. But to all who received him, who believed in his name, he gave power to become children of God.

—John 1:11, 12, RSV

Every time I read this passage I wonder how those people (even those in his own home!) could have been so blind and short-sighted as not to recognize who Jesus was. It is one of the tragedies of our confused and self-willed world that the only perfect Person who ever lived here would have been misunderstood and mistreated, and ultimately rejected completely. Yet I can't help wondering if the same reception might await him if he came again in the flesh. Would I acclaim him—would I offer him the hospitality of my home? Or would my heart, instead of being his home, be so preoccupied with earthly pursuits as to crowd him out?

For further reflection:
1. Would I recognize Jesus if he crossed my path today?
2. Is there room in my heart for Jesus—or do I allow other matters to crowd him out?

In the light of your presence, Lord, today I will:

For this reason a man shall leave his father and mother and be joined to his wife, and the two shall become one.

Ephesians 5:31, RSV

Psalm 68:6 says, "He [God] gives families to the lonely" (LB). This scripture applies beautifully to the Christian home. Somehow the home without God is missing a vital ingredient; we cannot enter fully into the true blessing of family living if our homes are not lifted up to God for his blessing. As husbands and wives live together in love and fidelity, as children "obey" their parents in the Lord, Christian homes grow in strength and beauty. In the sunlight of God's presence, the love of husband and wife, of parent and child, blooms into beauty and strength that natural impulse and mere circumstances cannot supply. Whatever else our homes must lack (for want of financial means), let us make sure they provide room for Christ's abiding love—for his name is Love!

For further reflection:
1. What place does Christ have in my home?
2. Who or what is placed above him?

Lord, today I open my home to be invaded by your presence. I will:

As thy days, so shall thy strength be.
                                        —Deuteronomy 33:25

We never have more than we can bear. The present hour we are always able to endure. As our day, so is our strength. If the trials of many years were gathered into one, they would overwhelm us; therefore, in pity to our little strength, He sends first one, and then another, then removes both, and lays on a third, heavier, perhaps, than either; but all is so wisely measured to our strength that the bruised reed is never broken. We do not enough look at our trials in this continuous and successive view. Each one is sent to teach us something, and altogether they have a lesson which is beyond the power of any to teach alone.

                          H. E. MANNING (1808–1892)

For further thought:
1. Is there a "trial" in my life right now?
2. What can I learn from it?

Lord, let me bear my trial knowing you are in charge. Today I will:

29 JULY

Read Psalm 5:1–3, 7, 8

Morning by morning, O Lord, you hear my voice; morning by morning I lay my requests before you and wait in expectation.

—Psalm 5:3, NIV

What a difference the way we begin our day makes! When we begin it with God—as the psalmist, David, does here—we find the way opening before us "in a fitting and orderly way" (1 Cor. 14:40, NIV). The path ahead seems bathed in light. Our responsibilities are seen in proper perspective. Our strength is sufficient for the day—indeed, it seems to be multiplied as the demands upon us increase. Even our leisure moments seem more fulfilling and refreshing. And the evening of the day is bathed in thankfulness and praise.

For further reflection:

1. How do I normally or customarily begin my day?
2. Do I lay my requests before God—and then wait in expectation?
3. What can I learn from David's prayer style here?

My prayer today to you, Lord, is:

He shall be as the light of the morning, when the sun riseth, even a morning without clouds, as the tender grass springing out of the earth by clear shining after rain.

—2 Samuel 23:4

What a beautiful description of a new day the dying King David gave here. Always the poet, even in his last words he painted a word picture of what it's like to receive the gift of a new day. Fresh from his eternity, God sends "a morning without clouds," a cloudless new day in which we may work and dream and pray. How priceless it is—and yet our Father sends it to us as a free gift of his love. We should carry the joy and song and radiance of this new morning into all the hours of the day. Later, clouds may gather, and outward circumstances may darken our day, but we are to keep the morning in our hearts and the song on our lips as we begin our tasks. As Jeremiah reminds us in Lamentations 3:23, our Lord's compassions are "new every morning: great is thy faithfulness." How thankful we should be for the freshness and beauty of each new day!

For further thought:
1. Can I greet each new day as David suggests here?
2. If I don't, does the fault lie in the day—or in me?

Lord, open my eyes to the opportunities of this new day. Today I will:

You shall have no other gods before me.

—Exodus 20:3, RSV

It is significant that if one only kept this, the first of the Ten Commandments, he would be able to keep them all—just as we would keep all if we fulfilled the eleventh commandment which Jesus left, "Love God, and love your neighbor as yourself." If idolatry (the practice this first commandment condemned) is putting something else before God in one's life, then avoiding idolatry will help me keep the rest of the commandments. If other "gods" get in the way, however, I've failed. What are some of these? Money, ambition, illicit sexual pleasure, and so on—they have one thing in common. Something or someone has been put in the place of God, who should be in first place.

For further thought:
1. Am I guilty of placing anything before God in my life?
2. What kind of "idols" tempt me to put God in second place?

Lord, today help me to put you first as I:

The steadfast love of the Lord never ceases, his mercies never come to an end; they are new every morning; great is thy faithfulness.
—Lamentations 3:22, 23, RSV

Are not many of us conscious that we are living far below our privileges? Do we not understand that we are not as good Christians, as rich in character, as fruitful in life, as we might be? Do we not know that there is a possible fulness of spiritual blessedness which we have not yet attained? Why is it? Is there any want in God, from whom all good gifts come? Is not the reason things, earthly things, which fill our hearts and leave but small room for Christ? We have not the hunger for righteousness, for holiness, and though there is abundance of provision close before us, yet our souls are starving. If we would have the abundant life which Christ wants to give us, we must empty out of our hearts the perishing trifles that fill them, and make room for the Holy Spirit. We must pray for spiritual hunger; for only to those who hunger comes the promise of filling and satisfying.

J. R. MILLER (1840–1912)

For further thought:
1. Do I fail to claim my privileges as a child of God?
2. Do I really hunger for the fulness Jeremiah speaks of in this passage?
3. Am I a full partaker in "the steadfast love of the Lord"?

To partake of your love in a special way, Lord, today I will:

2 AUGUST

Take heed unto thyself.

—1 Timothy 4:16

Two things are of the primary importance in our Christianity—the doctrine we hold and the life we live. The apostle Paul recognizes the necessity of paying attention to each: "Take heed unto thyself and unto the doctrine." In other words, it is not enough to make sure that our views are scriptural and our doctrines sound. We must be sound "in charity, in patience," and in practice.

To take heed to oneself does not mean that we should become self-centered and introspective. It *does* means that we should maintain a spirit of prayer and watchfulness—remembering that health of soul is as essential to the spiritual life as health of body is to the natural life. It is when we get "below par" physically that we are most susceptible to disease, because we then possess very little power of resistance. How true this is spiritually! There is such a thing as a poor spiritual condition—and where health of soul is wanting, every spiritual faculty is affected. Holding sound doctrine is not enough; we must strive to maintain a healthy spirit through a living, active faith in the Lord's Word and prompt obedience to his will.

For further thought:

1. Do I have a personal conviction concerning doctrinal matters?
2. Do my doctrinal convictions relate to my life?
3. Are there areas of my spiritual life that could be healthier?

Taking heed unto myself, today I will:

AUGUST 3

When ye shall have done all those things which are commanded you, say, We are unprofitable servants.

—Luke 17:10

Our Lord teaches us here that there is no inherent merit in obedience. Whatever our works may be, however unceasing and self-denying, they never make God our debtor. It is our duty and our privilege to serve him. He has a full claim on all we are, as well as on what we have. The powers and faculties of mind and body, the influence and opportunities we enjoy, and the time we have at our disposal are all gifts that come directly from him. With these we have to trade. "Occupy till I come." If at his return we can come to him, bringing ten or five pounds as the result of our trading, we will still have to say, "*Thy* pound hath gained" this profit. We cannot, even by our most devoted service, place God under any obligation to us. Those who serve God best receive far more than they can give.

For further thought:

1. Am I guilty of thinking I have done God a favor because I am serving him?
2. What am I doing currently to serve God?

Today I will:

4 AUGUST

God is in the midst of her; she shall not be moved; God will help her right early.

—Psalm 46:5, RSV

We enter a world of antagonism and opposition the moment we resolve at Christ's feet to be Christians, to be true men and women, to obey God, to forsake sin, to do our duty. There never comes an hour when we can live nobly without effort, without resisting wrong influences, without struggling against the power of temptation. It never gets easy to be a worthy and faithful Christian. Sometimes we are almost ready to give it all up and to cease our struggling; but we should remember that the spiritual nobleness and beauty after which we are striving can become ours only through this very struggling.

J. R. MILLER (1840–1912)

For further thought:
1. Am I living as though I am in "the stream of God's mercy" (v.4)?
2. Do spiritual muscles grow in the same way that physical muscles do?

To build spiritual muscles, today I:

But the wisdom from above is first pure, then peaceable, gentle, open to reason, full of mercy and good fruits, without uncertainty or insincerity.

—James 3:17, RSV

We are in no condition for good work of any kind when we are fretful and anxious in our minds. It is only when the peace of God is in our hearts that we are ready for true and helpful ministry. A feverish heart makes a worried face, and a worried face casts shadows wherever the person goes. A troubled spirit mars the temper and the disposition. It makes the whole life less beautiful. It unfits one for giving cheer and inspiration, for touching other lives with good and helpful impulses. Peace must come before ministry. It was when Jesus had touched the sufferer's hand and the fever had left her that she arose and ministered unto her friends.

J. R. MILLER (1840–1912)

For further thought:
1. Do I live up to the kind of character James is describing here?
2. Do I cast shadows or blessings wherever I go?

In the interest of peace, today I will:

6 AUGUST

I have glorified thee on the earth: I have finished the work which thou gavest me to do.

—John 17:4

Jesus is the supreme example of One who involved himself in tireless yet satisfying activity. He was divinely human in his attitude toward work. He found his rest not in ceasing to labor, but in ever-new forms of helpful service. We are unjust to him, and we rob ourselves of much of the inspiration and power of his life if we conceive that he was only *acting* a human role while in reality living above our human level in some detached and transcendent way. Without sacrificing any portion of his divinity, our Lord thoroughly identified himself with us in the great adventure of living. He met the same problems and temptations we meet, winning at last the victory which has to be the aim and goal of our lives.

For further thought:
1. Can I do my work with the same intensity and dedication Jesus did?
2. Does my work "glorify" my Father in heaven?
3. If I must answer either of these questions with a "no," do I need to think about a different kind of work involvement?

Lord, help me to place my work in proper perspective today by:

Trust in the Lord with all thine heart; and lean not unto thine own understanding.

—Proverbs 3:5

Have I ever said to myself, "I'll do this thing, but my heart really isn't in it"? Is this the way I tackle my daily tasks? If my heart isn't in it, then I'm acting merely out of a sense of duty or pressure. How much better it would be if I "trust in the Lord with all [my] heart." What a difference this would make in the *way* I did things—and in the attitude I show while doing it. Trust cannot be lightly placed in just anyone—but the Lord is certainly not only *worthy* of my trust, but eminently able to carry me through. My responsibility is to place myself where he can thus bless me!

For further thought:
1. Do I live my life and do my work wholeheartedly?
2. If not, why not?

To show my "trust" today I will:

8 AUGUST

Can ye drink of the cup that I drink of? and be baptized with the baptism that I am baptized with?

—Mark 10:38

The worst part of martyrdom is not the last agonizing moment; it is the wearing, daily steadfastness. Men who can make up their minds to hold out against the torture of an hour have sunk under the weariness and the harassment of small prolonged vexations. And there are many Christians who have the weight of some deep, incommunicable grief pressing, cold as ice, upon their hearts. To bear that cheerfully and manfully is to be a martyr. There is many a Christian bereaved and stricken in the best hopes of life. For such a one to say quietly, "Father, not as I will, but as Thou wilt," is to be a martyr. There is many a Christian who feels the irksomeness of the duties of life, and feels his spirit revolting from them. To get up every morning with the firm resolve to find pleasure in those duties, and do them well, and finish the work which God has given us to do, that is to drink Christ's cup. The humblest occupation has in it materials of discipline for the highest heaven.

F. W. ROBERTSON (1816–1853)

For further thought:
1. Do I know any "modern-day martyrs"?
2. Do I have an opportunity to experience even a "mild martyrdom"?

In the light of your example, Lord, today I will:

And Peter remembered the saying of Jesus, "Before the cock crows you will deny me three times." And he went out and wept bitterly.
—Matthew 26:75, RSV

There are many ways our lives can grieve the Lord—but certainly verbalizing a denial as Peter did here is one of the most apparent. What sorrow and repentance this should lead to. Like Paul, we leave undone the things we ought to do and we do those things we should not do (Rom. 7:19)—and we are ashamed of ourselves. But outright denial such as Peter did here—that is devastating. If our sin were but a violation of some formal law, or if we had no knowledge of a personal God manifested in Christ, who is grieved by our sin, we might be motivated to make a change in our *modus operandi*. But a shattering experience such as Peter had here must stir us to the very depths of our souls—the cleansing purge that would lead to a new life of faith. At Pentecost that new birth came to pass in Peter's life. Lord, send me a Pentecost!

For further consideration:
1. Have I ever denied Jesus as blatantly as Peter did here?
2. Do I sometimes do it in more subtle ways—but just as definitely?

Because denial comes in such subtle packages, Lord, today I will:

10 AUGUST

And Jesus, perceiving in himself that power had gone forth from him, immediately turned about in the crowd, and said, "Who touched my garments?"

—Mark 5:30, RSV

What a striking example of faith this is! The woman's belief that Jesus could heal her was implicit. She would not have tried to touch him if she hadn't believed he could heal her. And the remarkable thing is that healing occurred without any conscious action on the part of Jesus. All Jesus knew was that power had gone out of him. The woman had to come up and identify herself as the one who had touched him. At that point Jesus said, "Your faith has made you well" (v. 34). I can't help wondering—what if she had merely and inadvertently bumped against him in the crowd? Would she have been healed? I don't think so. Her faith made the difference. I wonder what my faith would have been in this situation. Would it have been as strong as the faith of this woman? And the Object of her faith made a tremendous difference too. If she had touched the garment of one of the disciples, it would have made no difference—but the Object of her faith had the power to heal her, and he did!

For further thought:
1. I wonder if this woman would have remained healed had she not come up to Jesus and "told him the whole truth" (v. 33).
2. Is there some physical or spiritual illness I should be sharing with Jesus?

Lord, today I bring you:

AUGUST 11

Am I my brother's keeper?

—Genesis 4:9

Which now of these three, thinkest thou, was neighbour unto him that fell among the thieves? And he said, He that shewed mercy on him. Then said Jesus unto him, Go, and do thou likewise.

—Luke 10:36, 37

How many are the sufferers who have fallen amongst misfortunes along the wayside of life! "By *chance*," we come that way; chance, accident, Providence, has thrown them in our way; we see them from a distance, like the Priest, or we come upon them suddenly, like the Levite; our business, our pleasure, is interrupted by the sight, is troubled by the delay; what are our feelings, what are our actions toward them? "Who is thy neighbor?" It is the sufferer, wherever, whoever, whatsoever he be. Wherever you hear the cry of distress, wherever you see anyone brought across your path by the chances and changes of life (that is, by the Providence of God), whom it is in your power to help—he, stranger or enemy though he be—*he* is your neighbor.

A. P. STANLEY (1815–1882)

For further thought:
1. Have I ever been a "good Samaritan"?
2. Is there a "brother" I should be "keeping" today?

Today I will be (or have been) a Good Samaritan to:

Show me thy ways, O Lord; teach me thy paths.

—Psalm 25:4

That which is often asked of God, is not so much His will and way, as His approval of our way.

S. F. SMILEY

There is nothing like the first glance we get at duty, before there has been any special pleading of our affections or inclinations. Duty is never uncertain at first. It is only after we have got involved in the mazes and sophistries of wishing that things were otherwise than they are, that it seems indistinct. Considering duty is often only explaining it away. Deliberation is often only dishonesty. God's guidance is plain, when we are true.

F. W. ROBERTSON (1816–1853)

For further thought:
1. Am I moving in *my* path or God's path for my life?
2. Have I ever asked God for his direction in my life—and have I received it?

Lord, today I perceive that my duty is:

Every one... who hears these words of mine and does them will be like a wise man who built his house upon the rock.
—Matthew 7:24, RSV

I have noticed that wherever there has been a faithful following of the Lord in a consecrated soul, several things have inevitably followed, sooner or later. Meekness and quietness of spirit become in time the characteristics of the daily life. A submissive acceptance of the will of God as it comes in the hourly events of each day; pliability in the hands of God to do or to suffer all the good pleasure of His will; sweetness under provocation; calmness in the midst of turmoil and bustle; yieldingness to the wishes of others, and an insensibility to slights and affronts; absence of worry or anxiety; deliverance from care and fear—all these, and many similar graces, are invariably found to be the natural outward development of that inward life which is hid with Christ in God.

H. W. Smith (1832–1911)

For further thought:
1. Am I a "doer" of the word as well as a "hearer"?
2. What do I need to do right now to show that I'm more than a "hearer"?

Lord, in obedience to your command today I will:

14 AUGUST

And Enoch walked with God: and he was not; for God took him.
—Genesis 5:24

Is it possible for any of us in these modern days to so live that we may walk with God? Can we walk with God in the shop, in the office, in the household, and on the street? When men exasperate us, and work wearies us, and the children fret, and the servants annoy, and our best-laid plans fall to pieces, and our castles in the air are dissipated like bubbles that break at a breath, then can we walk with God? That religion which fails us in the everyday trials and experiences of life has somewhere in it a flaw. It should be more than a plank to sustain us in the rushing tide, and land us exhausted and dripping on the other side. It ought if it come from above, to be always, day by day, to our souls as the wings of a bird, bearing us away from and beyond the impediments which seek to hold us down. If the Divine Love be a conscious presence, an indwelling force with us, it will do this.

CHRISTIAN UNION

For further thought:
1. Do I know anyone who "walks" with God as Enoch did?
2. What kind of a life would Enoch have lived today?

Today I will "walk with God" by:

Whither shall I go from thy Spirit? or whither shall I flee from thy presence?

Psalm 139:7

Where then is *our* God? You say, he is *everywhere:* then show me *anywhere* that you have met him. You declare him *everlasting:* then tell me *any moment* that he has been with you. You believe him ready to help them who are tempted, and to lift those who are bowed down: then in what passionate hour did you subside into his calm grace? In what sorrow lose yourself in his "more exceeding" joy? These are the testing questions by which we may learn whether we too have raised our altar to an "unknown God" and pay the worship of the blind; or whether we commune with him "in whom we live, and move, and have our being" (Acts 27:28).

J. Martineau (1805–1900)

For further thought:
1. How do I handle the questions in this meditation?
2. How *personally* can I identify with David in this psalm?

Lord, today I'd like to ask you:

Walk worthy of the Lord unto all pleasing, being fruitful in every good work, and increasing in the knowledge of God; Strengthened with all might, according to his glorious power, unto all patience and longsuffering with joyfulness.

—Colossians 1:10, 11

To shape the whole future is not our problem; but only to shape faithfully a small part of it, according to rules already known. It is perhaps possible for each of us, who will with due earnestness inquire, to ascertain clearly what he, for his own part, ought to do; this let him do with true heart, and continue doing. The general issue will, as it has always done, rest well with a Higher Intelligence than ours. This day I know ten commanded duties, see in my mind ten things which should be done for one that I do! I must do one of them; this of itself will show me ten others which can and shall be done.

THOMAS CARLYLE (1795–1880)

For further thought:
1. What *one* thing should I be doing today?
2. What am I doing in "my little corner of the world" that is significant and meaningful?

Lord, today I sense you are telling me:

Thou therefore endure hardness, as a good soldier of Jesus Christ.
—2 Timothy 2:3

Of nothing may we be more sure than this; that, if we cannot consecrate our present lot, we could make sacred no other. Our heaven and our Almighty Father are involved in our daily lives or nowhere. The obstructions of that lot are given for us to heave away by the concurrent touch of a holy spirit, and labor of strenuous will; its gloom for us to tint with some celestial light; its mysteries are for our worship; its sorrows for our trust; its perils for our courage; its temptations for our faith. Soldiers of the cross, it is not for us, but for our Leader and our Lord, to choose the field; it is ours, taking the station which he assigns, to make it the field of truth and honor, though it be the field of death.

J. MARTINEAU (1805–1900)

For further thought:
1. Am I obeying my Leader and Lord in my daily life?
2. Am I *consecrating* and *dedicating* my life's work to the cause of Christ?

Lord, today I yield myself to you as I:

18 AUGUST

In whom also we have obtained an inheritance, being predestinated according to the purpose of him who worketh all things after the counsel of his own will.

—Ephesians 1:11

We are apt to feel as if nothing we could do on earth bears a relation to what the good are doing in a higher world; but it is not so. Heaven and earth are not so far apart. Every disinterested act, every sacrifice to duty, every exertion for the good of "one of the least of Christ's brethren," every new insight into God's works, every new impulse given to the love of truth and goodness associates us with the departed, brings us nearer to them, and is as truly heavenly as if we were acting, not on earth, but in heaven. The spiritual tie between us and the departed is not felt as it should be. Our union with them daily grows stronger, if we daily make progress in what they are growing in.

WM. E. CHANNING (1780–1842)

For further thought:
1. Am I as "heavenly minded" as I should be?
2. What is my personal "inheritance" from those who have gone before me?

Today, I feel especially close to _____ **, who has gone on before. I will:**

Whether therefore ye eat, or drink, or whatsoever ye do, do all to the glory of God.

—1 Corinthians 10:31

Our thoughts, good or bad, are not in our command, but every one of us has at all hours duties to do, and these he can do negligently, like a slave, or faithfully, like a true servant. "Do the duty that is nearest thee"—that first, and that well; all the rest will disclose themselves with increasing clearness, and make their successive demand. Were your duties never so small, I advise you, set yourself with double and treble energy and punctuality, to do them hour after hour, day after day.

THOMAS CARLYLE (1795–1880)

Whatever we are, high or lowly, learned or unlearned, married or single, in a full house or alone, charged with many affairs or dwelling in quietness, we have our daily round of work, our duties of affection, obedience, love, mercy, industry, and the like; and that which makes one man to differ from another is not so much what things he does, as his manner of doing them.

H. E. MANNING (1808–1892)

For further thought:
1. Am I living as Paul admonishes here in 1 Corinthians— doing "all to the glory of God"?
2. Is there anything in my life that I need to set right?

In light of this exhortation, today I will:

Forgetting those things which are behind, and reaching forth unto those things which are before, I press toward the mark for the prize of the high calling of God in Christ Jesus.

—Philippians 3:13, 14

It is not by regretting what is irreparable that true work is to be done, but by making the best of what we are. It is not by complaining that we have not the right tools, but by using well the tools we have. What we are, and where we are, is God's providential arrangement—God's doing, though it may be man's misdoing; and the manly and the wise way is to look our disadvantages in the face, and see what can be made out of them. Life, like war, is a series of mistakes, and he is not the best Christian nor the best general who makes the fewest false steps. He is the best who wins the most splendid victories by the retrieval of mistakes. Forget mistakes; organize victory out of mistakes.

F. W. ROBERTSON (1816–1853)

For further thought:
1. What "mistakes" do I need to forget?
2. What goals should I strive for?

My "goal" for today is to:

I have been crucified with Christ; it is no longer I who live, but Christ who lives in me; and the life I now live in the flesh I live by faith in the Son of God, who loved me and gave himself for me.
—Galatians 2:20, RSV

Paul is pretty hard on Peter in this passage, but he verbalizes a truth about the Christ-filled life that I need to remember. One of the sharpest contrasts between Christianity and other religious faiths lies in the area of the indwelling presence of the risen Christ. No other faith offers anything comparable to it—Christ in us, the secret of Christianity's power in our lives and in the world. Or, as Paul puts it in Colossians 1:27, "Christ in you the hope of glory." Through his intimate possession of our hearts and wills, our characters are transformed. The old self dies, and the new self with new hope, new loyalties, new strength, and new enthusiasm arises in its place. My faith in Jesus is only partial as long as I think of him merely as an historic figure. Rather, he is still and forevermore in this world—and his abode is the heart of every one of his people.

For further thought:
1. Am I living as though the One who made me lives in my heart?
2. Am I guilty of "putting God in a box" of history?

With Paul I give my life totally to Christ today as I:

22 AUGUST

Train up a child in the way he should go, and when he is old, he will not depart from it.

—Proverbs 22:6

Contrary to popular opinion, wisdom doesn't necessarily come as a result of personal effort. Rather, it comes according to the unique economy of God. Life offers its best truths not to the sophisticated, but to the childlike heart. This is a comfort to some, a disillusionment to others—it depends upon one's perspective. A man may be very knowledgable so far as scientific technology is concerned, but woefully ignorant in terms of spirituality. Jesus said, "Except ye . . . become as little children, ye shall not enter [see] the kingdom of heaven" (Matt. 18:3). The greatest faith is also the simplest.

For further consideration:
1. Have I "seen myself" in these scriptures?
2. Do I come as a little child—or as a sophisticated adult?

Lord, may I have a childlike faith today as I:

Now we know that if the earthly tent we live in is destroyed, we have a building from God, an eternal house in heaven, not built by human hands. Meanwhile, we groan, longing to be clothed with our heavenly dwelling.

—2 Corinthians 5:1, 2, NIV

It is very easy, in the midst of our busy schedules, to fall into the trap of thinking that our lives consist of those things which we can see, which we can accumulate. When life seems most full of earthly joy and temporal satisfaction, that is the time we should pause to contemplate life immortal and eternal. The reason for this should not be to counteract our natural zest for this life, but actually to increase it—to allow the light of Eternity to illuminate our present way. To me as a Christian, Paul's thought of "an eternal house in heaven, not built by human hands," not resting upon the unsteady, unsure foundation man can construct, is a thought that inspires joy and fills my heart with hope and song. As Paul promises in verses 6 through 9, this is the reason that "we are always confident and know that as long as we are at home in the body we are away from the Lord. We live by faith, not by sight. We are confident, I say, and would prefer to be away from the body and at home with the Lord. So we make it our goal to please him...."

For further thought:
1. Do I take sufficient time to look "inside myself" and assess my inner attitudes?
2. On what kind of a foundation have I built my "earthly home"?

In the light of this promise, today I will:

24 AUGUST

On the morning of the third day there were thunders and lightnings, in a thick cloud upon the mountain, and a very loud trumpet blast, so that all the people who were in the camp trembled.

—Exodus 19:16, RSV

God speaks to his people in more than one way. Here he spoke loudly and with spectacular overtones. In 1 Kings 19:12 he spoke to Elijah in a "still small voice" after rejecting such vehicles as high wind and earthquake. We may hear God's voice in the sudden and the spectacular events of our lives—but it is just as probable that he will speak to us in the silence, quietly conveying to us the message he wants us to receive. He comes to us in the unusual, the shocking, the cataclysmic, and the catastrophic. But he also makes his presence known in gentler ways: by the quiet nudging of conscience, the steady glow of conviction—or by the constant remembrance of our first meeting with the Master.

For further consideration:

1. Am I listening both for the thunders and the silences?
2. Is my prayer life such that God can speak to me—or do I do all the talking and fail to listen for his voice?

Lord, today I will open my heart and life to you and I will:

For in this hope we were saved. But hope that is seen is no hope at all. Who hopes for what he already has? But if we hope for what we do not yet have, we wait for it patiently.

—Romans 8:24, 25, NIV

The creative power of hope is tremendous! To use the idiom of the King James Version, it brings to pass things that are not. Life's best realities begin by being hoped for. After being initiated by hope, they move to take on form and substance. This is especially true in the higher dimensions of living—the intellectual, moral, and spiritual. In these areas it is possible to do almost anything we want to with our lives. To desire greater intelligence, a nobler character, a deeper walk with Christ is, in a measure, to actually achieve that goal. Daring to hope for strength, wisdom, character—even immortality—is to reach out for those things confidently and competently. In a sense, we will discover when we possess them, that their reality depended all along upon our hope that they might be true. As the New Testament writer says, "Now faith is being sure of what we hope for and certain of what we do not see" (Heb. 11:1, NIV).

For further consideration:
1. Can my outlook be classified as "hopeful"?
2. On what do I rest my faith?

My hope for today is:

26 AUGUST

He ... preserveth the way of his saints.

—Proverbs 2:8

For he shall give his angels charge over thee, to keep thee in all thy ways.

—Psalm 91:11

God promises to keep both the ways and the feet of his saints: "He will guard the feet of his faithful ones" (1 Sam. 2:9, RSV). How little we realize our continual need of his preserving grace! It is not only the deliverance of our souls from death that we need God to accomplish. Even after we have realized that blessing, we need his power perpetually to keep our feet from stumbling.

We may think of "the way" as the path along which we have to travel—the way of holy obedience. God prepares it and preserves it. Along that path we will find the "good works, which God hath before ordained that we should walk in them" (Eph. 2:10). One great business of life is to be kept constantly "prepared unto every good work" (2 Tim. 2:21). This also God undertakes to do, if we are willing to give ourselves into his hand for this purpose. We need not be anxious as to our future—marking out our path and planning our ways. We have but to seek his guidance, and daily to be taught his way concerning us. He will say unto us, "This is the way; walk ye in it" (Isa. 30:21).

For further thought:
1. Do I depend upon God for daily guidance as I should?
2. When is the last time God told me, "This is the way; walk ye in it"?

Lord, today guide me to:

Thou hast cast all my sins behind thy back.

—Isaiah 38:17

Behind God's back where they could be seen no more—that is where Hezekiah said God had placed his sins. Hezekiah knew he had sinned; he regarded his sins as having brought down upon him the sentence of death. But as God had revoked the sentence, Hezekiah knew God had pardoned his sins and put them away from his remembrance.

God uses two other very striking figures to show the completeness of his pardon. He casts our sins into the depths of the sea (Micah 7:19), and "as far as the east is from the west, so far hath he removed our transgressions from us" (Ps. 103:12). Then he declares, concerning those forgiven sins, that he will remember them no more (Isa. 43:25).

But how may we live in the assurance of sins forgiven, in the light of his pardon? The apostle John tells us in 1 John 1:9: "If we confess our sins, he is faithful and just to forgive us our sins, and to cleanse us from all unrighteousness."

For further thought:
1. Do I believe this fact of forgiveness as unquestioningly as Hezekiah did?
2. Do I make it a daily practice to confess my sins to God?

Lord, today I confess:

28 AUGUST

The living God, who giveth us richly all things to enjoy.
—1 Timothy 6:17

We see from the context that the apostle charges Timothy to warn those "who are rich in this world" of their peril. "Charge them," he says, "not to be highminded" or haughty. Pride may be found without wealth; but it is difficult to have wealth without pride. Instead of trusting in wealth, the apostle would say, "Let us trust in the living God, to whom all riches belong, and who is the Giver of every good gift. It is he who gives us richly all things to enjoy. It is God's will, therefore, that we should accept his gifts— earthly as well as spiritual—and enjoy them as bestowed by his loving hand." "All things are yours," says the same apostle in another Epistle (1 Cor. 3:21).

How often we forget that the God who has redeemed our souls and supplies our spiritual needs is the God who provides all our temporal blessings!

He gives us all things to *enjoy.* God delights in the happiness of his children. It is when they take his gifts and forget the God who gave them that his name is dishonored.

For further thought:
1. Am I living as though God has given me "richly all things to enjoy"?
2. What keeps me from living my life up to its full potential of joy?

As I look at my life, today I will:

I will remember the works of the Lord: surely I will remember thy wonders of old. I will meditate also on all thy work, and talk of thy doings.

—Psalm 77:11, 12

There is nothing more needed in this agitated age than quiet times to be alone with God. It is not simply to make our requests known unto God that we come into his presence. We come to hear his voice. We come to learn his will. As we meditate on his Word, we are sowing the seeds of future action. It is as we submit our hearts and minds to the truth of his Word that we become possessed by it, and conformed to the image of his Son. Jeremiah says, "Thy words were found, and I did eat them" (15:16). It is only by quiet and prayerful meditation that this spiritual assimilation takes place. Then follows what the prophet records: "And thy word was unto me the joy and rejoicing of mine heart." We cannot all go into the field like Isaac and meditate (Gen. 24:63), but, as one has said, "the Lord is in the town, too, and will meet with you in your homes or in the crowded street. Let your heart go out to meet him."

For further thought:
1. Do I take as much time for meditation as I do for prayer?
2. Does God's Word have the proper place of prominence in my life?

Lord, today I will let your Word possess me as I:

Behold the Lamb of God.

—John 1:29

This was John the Baptist's first testimony to his disciples when he saw Jesus coming toward him. It is the first view of Christ that my sin-burdened soul needs. Christ the Sin-bearer must be seen before Christ as God's ideal of holiness can be followed. He is the Lamb of God bearing away the sin of the world. Isaiah says: "The Lord hath laid on him the iniquity of us all" (53:6). We see him doing the Father's will in putting away sin by the sacrifice of himself (Heb. 9:26). "Lo, I come to do thy will, O God" (Heb. 10:9). "By the which will we are sanctified through the offering of the body of Jesus Christ once for all" (verse 10). In that death we see God's will fulfilled, the world's sin atoned for, and the power of Satan overthrown.

This was no afterthought in the scheme of redemption. For Jesus is the Lamb slain before the foundation of the world (Rev. 13:8). Behold him! There is life in a look at the Crucified One. Adore him! "Worthy is the Lamb that was slain to receive power, and riches, and wisdom, and strength, and honour, and glory, and blessing" (Rev. 5:12).

For further thought:

1. What does it mean to me personally that Jesus is "the Lamb of God"?
2. Am I "bearing witness" that Jesus is "the Son of God" by my life and lip?

Because of what the Lamb of God has done for me, today I will:

Consider how great things he hath done for you.

1 Samuel 12:24

A consideration of God's past mercies strengthens our faith in his future blessings, and deepens our sense of present unworthiness. We lose a great deal by failing to take time for thoughtful consideration. The remembrance of what he has already done for us, and prayerful meditation on these facts, will dispel our doubts and turn our days of clouds and darkness into sunshine. There is divine logic in the reasoning: "He that spared not his own Son, but delivered him up for us all, how shall he not with him also freely give us all things?" (Rom. 8:32).

It is impossible to grasp the extent or to estimate the value of those gifts God has already bestowed, but we may "consider" them. Let us cultivate this habit of holy and devout meditation on the "great things" God has done for us. Doing so will deepen our thankfulness and quicken the spirit of prayer. "Bless the Lord, O my soul, and *forget not* all his benefits" (Ps. 103:1, italics mine).

For further thought:
1. How often do I take time to contemplate God's goodness to me and to my family?
2. What would a daily practice of this habit do to my life?

Because of the "great things" you have done for me, Lord, today I will:

... In every thing by prayer and supplication with thanksgiving let your requests be made known unto God.

—Philippians 4:6

The apostle Paul is warning the Philippian church—and all Christians—against anxiety. "Be careful for nothing." Be not anxious concerning anything. "But in everything by prayer," and so on. This is one of the means by which we can guard against worry. I can turn my trouble or anxiety into prayer. My prayer must be definite and specific. It must be earnest and full of praise. The remembrance of past mercies not only will strengthen my faith and lead me to expect future blessings; it will also help me to be more real and childlike in prayer. A special promise belongs to this precept, and follows it immediately: "And the peace of God, which passeth all understanding, shall keep your hearts and minds through Christ Jesus" (v. 7).

It is in vain we pray to be kept free from worry if we neglect to obey the Lord's direction. The burdens and cares that come upon us daily we must commit unto the Lord daily. It is as we fulfil that condition that we shall find the truth of the promise. God will surely fulfil his own undertaking, but he expects us to be obedient to his will.

For further consideration:
1. Can anxiety and thankfulness live side by side in me?
2. What is my usual frame of mind when I pray?

In the light of Paul's admonition here, today I will:

His commandments are not burdensome.

                                           —1 John 5:3, RSV

Why is it that many of us think God's commandments are a burden?

Well, some might say, because such people have never been "born again." To those who are unrenewed, all God's requirements are irksome. True, but how is it that even many who *have* been converted to God, who *have* been born of the Spirit, often find his commandments hard and burdensome? We must seek the answer not only in a new nature, but also in a right disposition of heart. This, in addition to the new nature, is essential to all happy and harmonious walking with God along the line of his will.

It is when our wills are not thoroughly in harmony with God's will that we experience his requirements as burdensome. Here, then, is a useful test for ascertaining our true spiritual condition. How do I regard God's commandments? Do I take the comfort of his promises, while at the same time I seek to turn aside from his commands?

To be in a right condition of soul is to find as much liberty and encouragement in what God requires of us as we find in what he bestows on us.

For further meditation:
1. Have I "heard" God's commandments lately?
2. Have I found them burdensome?

Lord, today I will:

We who are strong ought to bear with the failings of the weak, and not to please ourselves.

—Romans 15:1, RSV

Paul here echoes the message Jesus spoke throughout the Gospels—and the words are reminiscent of his admonition in Galatians 6:2: "Bear ye one another's burdens, and so fulfil the law of Christ." In Acts 20:35 Paul reminds his listeners, "In all things I have shown you that by so toiling one must help the weak, remembering the words of the Lord Jesus, how he said, 'It is more blessed to give than to receive.'"

Christ's law of unselfish service will always be a heavy yoke so long as it rests *upon* my will and not *within* my will. But when my soul has organized itself to include others as an essential part of itself, so as to root unselfish service in the very will to live, then the will to serve is no longer a burdening yoke but an inherent joy. This, perhaps, is one meaning of conversion—a thorough and radical rearrangement of lifestyle which enlarges one's self to include other selves as an essential part of it. The will to serve involves the will to put others before one's self, so that we "bear... one another's burdens, and so fulfil the law of Christ."

For further thought:
1. Do I serve others from selfish or unselfish motives?
2. Is my lifestyle conducive to serving others?

As an expression of my love, today I will:

SEPTEMBER 4

Walk in love.

—Ephesians 5:2

Love is the power that has drawn us as sinners unto God, that has melted the hardness of our hearts, and that now constrains us to live for him. Love is the sphere of the Christian's activity. "God is love; and he that dwelleth in love dwelleth in God, and God in him" (1 John 4:16). We are called to be followers, imitators of God. Therefore we have to "walk in love."

"God for Christ's sake hath forgiven you." If we imitate God in this respect we shall forgive one another. The apostle makes no distinction between our being the objects of God's love and our being the objects of the love of Christ. It is one and the same love. We have not only to contemplate and rejoice in this love, we have to "walk" in it. That is, we have to show it in a practical way; we have to exemplify it. "Walking" is the term which the apostle uses to point out the practical side of Christianity. As with our bodies, so with our souls, we need exercise, in order to develop fully as God would have us do. We cannot remain healthy unless we are carrying out into practice that which we have received as the cardinal truths of our faith.

For further meditation:

1. What does it mean, from a practical point of view, to "walk in love"?
2. Is it possible to "imitate" God?

Today I will show that I "walk in love" by:

Seek those things which are above, where Christ sitteth on the right hand of God.

—Colossians 3:1

This exhortation is based on the fact that, as believers, we are risen with Christ. To be risen with Christ means that in God's sight we are translated into heaven. Bishop Lightfoot explains it this way: "All your aims must [therefore,] center in heaven, where reigns the Christ who has thus exalted you, enthroned on God's right hand. All your thoughts must abide in heaven, not on the earth. For, I say it once again, you have nothing to do with mundane things; you *died*—died once for all to the world; you are living another life. This life, indeed, is hidden now; it has not outward splendour as men count splendour; for it is a life with Christ, a life in God."

It is human nature to seek that which we love and delight in. It is where our treasure is that our heart will be also. "Whom have I in heaven but thee? and there is none upon earth that I desire besides thee." What are the things that we seek? We seek after those things that are filling our thoughts and attracting our affections. Upon these we set our wills and concentrate our energies. It is not difficult to seek what we love.

For further meditation:
1. What am I "seeking" in life?
2. Is it natural for me to look heavenward—or do I tend to be earthbound?

Looking above, today I will:

The Lord loveth the righteous.

—Psalm 146:8

Most of us have times when we can say, "Oh, I know that God loves me now"; but the feeling is transient, and soon passes away. Tomorrow we are doubting and fearing as before, and the joy has gone out of our heart. Does God's love, then, change? Did he love me yesterday, and does he not love me today? Has the divine heart unclasped its hold upon me? No; the love of God is changeless and eternal. Heaven and earth may pass away, but the kindness of the Lord shall never depart from any of his children. Let us try to grasp this truth. Then, come what may, joy or sorrow, prosperity or adversity, we shall know always that the love of God abides unchanging—that we are held in its clasp with a hold that never can be torn loose.

J. R. MILLER (1840–1912)

For further thought:
1. Does God's love rest on his faithfulness or my righteousness?
2. As I think upon God's steadfast love, what effect should this have on my attitude toward my circumstances and the things that happen to me?

In the light of your love, Lord, today I will:

7 SEPTEMBER

Wherefore, O King Agrippa, I was not disobedient to the heavenly vision.

—Acts 26:19, RSV

Paul's conversion experience illustrates the gift or the power some have to see with the inward eye—the ability to see the invisible, as it were. There is given to us the power of seeing with an inner eye by intuition, by a kind of instinct. Thus our soul has a way of divining truth and reality without much apparent help from formal reason. This power lies within our imagination, which is the power wherein lodges also the genius of all creative people—poets, artists, prophets, and makers of song. In a way, it is through our imagination that God is continually creating for us a new world—new heavens and a new earth. The vista of eternity opens up to us as we see reality through the eyes of the imagination.

For further consideration:
1. What have I seen lately through the eyes of my imagination?
2. Is my imagination self-centered or God-centered?

My spiritual instinct tells me to:

He answered, "Whether he is a sinner, I do not know; one thing I know, that though I was blind, now I see."

—John 9:25, RSV

Someone has said that experience is the best teacher. That is the way we gain much of our knowledge. How little we learn by sheer reasoning compared to what we learn by experience! There are depths of conviction and assurance in our hearts which reasoning could not attain and may *never* attain. This is not to rob reason of its proper place. The intellect is the structure around which we fashion our way of life. But I must keep clear in my mind that reality is more than my philosophy of it, that life overflows the intellectual container in which I try to capture it. Thank God, the power of Christ can heal and comfort and save my soul, even though I am unable to give a rational explanation of how it is all accomplished. Experience is often instinctive in its understanding, rather than intellectual. That's the way this blind man understood Jesus—and his insight far exceeded that of the learned Jews around him.

For further thought:
1. Where should I place myself—with the Jews or with the blind man—in respect to my attitude toward Jesus?
2. Is my understanding of who Jesus is instinctive or intellectual?

The "one thing I know" right now is:

9 SEPTEMBER

Thou visitest the earth and waterest it, thou greatly enrichest it; the river of God is full of water; thou providest their grain, for so thou hast prepared it.

—Psalm 65:9, RSV

David here reminds me of a truth I often overlook: the blessings of each day are the gifts of God. In earlier times—or perhaps even today, if I were working directly with the land and saw his "bounty" in the sun and the rain—I might not need such frequent reminders of his goodness. His blessings are too numerous to mention—and probably the best gift of all is a sensitivity to his presence. He ministers to our spirits in both the good and the bad that come. Our misfortunes, though not sent of God, are a part of the discipline by which we are educated for eternity. Therefore, we display the highest quality of gratitude if, in counting our blessings, we see our hardships and burdens in their true light as part of his providence for our benefit and growth.

For further thought:

1. Am I "enduring" a problem now that could turn out to be a blessing?
2. As I see God's hand in nature, do I also sense it in my own life?

Today I see the following blessings in my burdens and in nature around me:

As a father pities his children, so the Lord pities those who fear him.
—Psalm 103:13, RSV

I am beginning to understand how some have difficulty picturing God as a loving father—for some have never even known a father, let alone a *loving* father. It is easier for them to picture God as a wrathful behemoth, towering above them in a rage because of their sins. But David here pictures God as Jesus did in the parable of the prodigal son—as One standing with open arms of forgiveness to welcome his errant child home from his wanderings. We cannot hold God's majesty in too great awe. But it is possible for us to hold his greatness in such awe that we do not allow our souls intimacy with him. This he craves, and this we need. The one great fact Jesus came to reveal was that the infinite and eternal God is all-loving too. He is a tender Father as well as a mighty Ruler. To keep our intimacy free from irreverence and our awe free from cold formality is to find the open way to true and satisfying communion with God.

For further thought:
1. What is my "inner picture" of God—forgiving Father, or forbidding Judge, or something else?
2. Have I thought to thank him today that his true nature is love?

Lord, I know you are my Father because:

11 SEPTEMBER

Read 1 Peter 5:1–7

... All of you be subject one to another, and be clothed with humility: for God resisteth the proud, and giveth grace to the humble.
—1 Peter 5:5

Success is as prone to pull us down as it is to lift us up. It takes only a little prosperity to fill us with a false sense of self-confidence that forgets God and clouds the true values of life. A delicate line falls between the secular self-confidence and the serenity of true humility. Some, in error, identify humility with a lack of self-regard, a subservience in attitude which harms the personality and hinders relationships with others. True humility is consistent with sound self-consideration. It is the grace of seeing oneself in proper perspective—in a relationship with others that frees one to have full respect for their personalities as well as one's own. True humility frees one to both give and receive service from others without egotism or servility. "Better it is to be of a humble spirit with the lowly, than to divide the spoil..." (Prov. 16:9).

For further thought:
1. How do I see "humility" in the light of the "fruit of the Spirit" listed in Galatians 5:22, 23?
2. Who should be my pattern for humility—from the Bible, from among my contemporaries?
3. Do I have a problem with pride?

Lord, today help me to yield to you as I:

SEPTEMBER 12

For I know my transgressions and my sin is ever before me.
—Psalm 51:3, RSV

Secret sins are perhaps the most difficult to deal with. Publicity tends to shame us into forsaking the more obvious transgressions of God's law—but hidden sins flourish in the dark corners of our lives. The consciousness that our fault is known to one other mind beside our own tends to deepen our repentance and to strengthen our own soul. Unobserved and unsuspected by others, the secret sins of temper, pride, uncharitableness, and sensuality work disaster. Because they are so easily concealed, they make themselves at home within us. We need to pray, as David did here in Psalm 51, that God would restore unto us the "joy of our salvation," as we expose our inner lives to his cleansing. We need to pray, as Moses did in Psalm 90, "Thou hast set our iniquities before thee, our secret sins in the light of thy countenance" (v. 8).

For further thought:
1. What "secret sin" am I cherishing?
2. Do I dare to pray as David did in verse 3, "wash me..."?
3. What was David's sin?

In prayer, dear Lord, I confess to you:

... So will I save you and ye shall be a blessing: fear not, but let your hands be strong.

—Zechariah 8:13

The Christian life, while not realized in Zechariah's day, was at least recognized as the life of faith. Throughout its course, whether brief or broad, life offers us a clarion call to achievement and accomplishment. The Bible assumes that true success is always possible to those who have faith and who make the effort. There are vast resources of divine help at the service of those who would claim them.

Fear is the opposite of faith; it is the archenemy of achievement. It paralyzes initiative and renders the soul short-sighted. No true estimate of its resources can be made by a soul seized with fear. But to the man of courage and vision the mountains roundabout are always full of potential for God. "For God hath not given us the spirit of fear; but of power, and of love, and of a sound mind" (2 Timothy 1:7).

For further thought:
1. Is my life dominated by fear or faith?
2. In what area of life do my fears lie?

Lord, I pray that fear will be removed from my life and be replaced by faith. By faith I want to:

And the barrel of meal wasted not, neither did the cruse of oil fail, according to the word of the Lord which he spake by Elijah.
—1 Kings 17:16

One of the things I've learned as I've grown older is that my basic, real *needs* are relatively few. Most of my unhappiness comes from craving things I do not need. True wisdom is found in the grateful acceptance of the simpler blessings and a deep desire to become rich in mind and heart. I'm afraid, in my case, that too often these are the most lavishly bestowed but the least regarded of all the gifts God gives me.

My life is sheltered by God's providence, which brings me every good and perfect gift. As my life goes on, I learn to expect less of the world, for it is only on the worldly side that many of my dreams fail to be realized. I find God's grace unfailing, and his blessings are the daily supply of his mercy. These prove enough for my comfort and happiness.

For further thought:
1. Do I live as if God were supplying my needs—or as if this were my responsibility?
2. What would be the modern equivalents of "the barrel of meal" and the "cruse of oil"?

Lord, help me to be content with what you supply and give me a grateful heart so that I can:

15 SEPTEMBER

And therefore will the Lord wait, that he may be gracious unto you, and therefore will he be exalted, that he may have mercy upon you: for the Lord is a God of judgment: blessed are all they that wait for him.

—Isaiah 30:18

Waiting is a real discipline for me. Tarrying in calmness until God speaks to me is not one of my virtues! For me, waiting requires a higher order of faith than does action. After I've done my part, if God seems slack in putting things in motion, I find my faith "strangely tested." I need to learn that waiting is a natural and necessary part of spiritual growing. I must remember that my silence can honor God as well as my speech. My restful repose is just as important as my activity. Patient preparation to act is more vital than hasty and ill-conceived actions. Such faith, such calm patience, never loses its reward. "Blessed are all they that wait for him"!

For further thought:
1. Am I doing better at the waiting game than I used to?
2. If not, is there some discipline that would help me gain this patience?

Lord, make me more patient by:

Search me, oh God, and know my heart! Try me and know my thoughts!

—Psalm 139:23, RSV

Would I dare pray a prayer like this? Here David is turning over the rights to his inner life to God. In effect, he is simply giving God a search warrant into his very soul! I realize that God knows my thoughts whether I want him to or not—but that realization is far short of David's honest and transparent prayer, opening himself completely to God. It reminds me of Job's claim to integrity in Job 31:6. He, too, opened himself to God, and because of that openness God blessed him abundantly—more so in his later life than in his earlier, seemingly more prosperous days. Jesus, too, encountered those who opened themselves to him: men like Nathaniel, women like Mary Magdalene. These, too, gave God a search warrant into the privacy of their inner hearts—and cleansing was the result.

For further thought:
1. Have I ever asked God to "search me"?
2. If I did, what would he find?

Lord, I need the cleansing you can give. Help me today to deal with:

17 SEPTEMBER

Read 1 John 2:15–17

And the world passes away, and the lust of it; but he who does the will of God abides forever.

—1 John 2:17, RSV

The apostle John had tremendous insight into spiritual truths, gained through his earthly walk with Jesus and the things he learned at the feet of the Holy Spirit after Jesus ascended. One primary truth he learned: Nothing can have real value that does not last. Much that is captivating in life has this fundamental limitation—it doesn't endure. To learn to distinguish between the things that pass and the things that abide is the secret of true wisdom and happiness. While the things that pass away are accessible to the few, God has so ordered his world that enduring things, the invaluable things of character, grace, and immortality, are open to us all and may be had for the asking. What abides forever is available to all regardless of station in life or size of bank account.

For further thought:
1. What things of the "world" do I love too much?
2. Do I know what it means to live in "the will of God"?

Lord, desiring your will for my life, today I will:

This is the day which the Lord has made; let us rejoice and be glad in it.

—Psalm 118:24, RSV

Often this verse (24) is used to set the mood for a Sunday morning worship service—but it's a perfect slogan for every day. God's goodness is disclosed to us in his many provisions for fresh beginnings on the great adventure of life. Our souls are often confused and entangled in their own misdirections, like sheep who have lost their way and been caught in the thicket. Instead of leaving us in our hopelessness, God sets us on the path again. Through nature and the ordinary round of life his divine goodness presents us with ever-new opportunities. Sleep blots out much of the trouble and confusion of the day, and with the coming of dawn we stand at a fresh beginning unencumbered by yesterday's burden. The Lord's day brings us a similar new departure in our week of days. It is a chance to freshen our vision, to "gird up" our loins again, and to grip our unfinished tasks with renewed zeal and enthusiasm.

For further thought:
1. What would my day be like if it began with the evening?
2. What would happen to my day without the regular night's rest that precedes it?

Lord, thank you again for each new day—and especially for the Lord's day. Let me use today for your glory as I:

19 SEPTEMBER

For since, in the wisdom of God, the world did not know God through wisdom, it pleased God through the folly of what we preach to save those who believe.

—1 Corinthians 1:21, RSV

There are some "intellectuals" who consider the message of Christ and the gospel to be "folly." They look up to the "wisdom of men" and down upon the "foolishness of God" (v. 25). The first Christians were a laughing stock to the intellectuals of their day—and there are still those who disparage the gospel and elevate the world's wisdom. Wherever self-confidence and intellectual arrogance have prevailed, there the message of the cross has been discounted—for a time. But those who have learned its secret have another conviction—they are the ones who "boast of the Lord." They alone know true wisdom and peace, calm assurance and restful trust. Undergirded by that "wisdom from above," they enter into life with joy and confidence in God instead of in self.

For further thought:
1. Where is my confidence placed—in God or self?
2. What do I consider wisdom?

Lord, I look to you for true wisdom. Help me today to:

And Jacob was left alone; and there wrestled a man with him until the breaking of the day.

—Genesis 32:24

God is graciously willing to answer our prayers. But there are still times in each of our lives when our prayers become a virtual wrestling match with God. It is as if we are struggling with the divine will for the mastery. To each of us there comes that moment of crisis when it is difficult to wait for God's will to come clear. We find no relief, and cry out to God for deliverance. We are like Jacob, unwilling to let our heavenly Wrestler go. It is in such hours that our merciful heavenly Father makes himself known to us, and when the dawn comes we can look into his face, knowing from past experience that he will hear and answer us.

For further thought:
1. Are any of my prayers "wrestling" prayers?
2. Does God always expect a carefully structured prayer—or is it okay to "wrestle" with him at times?

Lord, today I'm wrestling with:

Therefore, put on the full armor of God, so that when the day of evil comes you may be able to stand your ground, and after you have done everything, to stand. Stand firm, then, with the belt of truth buckled around your waist, with the breastplate of righteousness in place, and with your feet fitted with the readiness that comes from the gospel of peace.

—Ephesians 6:13–15, NIV

There is a kind of "standing" or waiting which is nothing more than idleness and inactivity—the expedient reaction of an unprepared, hesitant, and wavering nature. But there is also a kind of resolute waiting which results in self-preparation. This is the kind of active waiting that culminates in the "girded loin" and the "watchful spirit." Such preparation readies the "waiter" for action rather than dulling his senses to the world around him. This kind of waiting is a kind of service—a spiritual alertness that prepares one for obedience to the heavenly call.

For further thought:
1. What kind of "waiting" or "standing" characterizes my life?
2. What does it mean to have on "the belt of truth" and "the breastplate of righteousness"?

Lord, I need to learn the lesson of quietness and obedience. Help me today to:

In the days of his flesh, Jesus offered up prayers and supplications, with loud cries and tears, to him who was able to save him from death, and he was heard for his godly fear.

—Hebrews 5:7, RSV

If we have an idea that Jesus' temptation was a mere facade—that it amounted to a mere pageant of victory—we have really misread the biblical account. If Jesus was somehow by his very nature above and apart from the downward pull and evil of the world around him, then his experience means little to those of us who struggle with the nitty-gritty of life, every day of our lives. But it is comforting to know past all certainty that he won his victory through struggle, even as we must do. Into the shadow of his sorrow and agony it is our privilege and right to enter, that with him we may emerge cleansed and victorious by the grace of God.

For further thought:
1. Do I ever pray with "crying and tears"?
2. If Jesus prayed this way, should I expect to be exempted?

Lord, today I bring you this concern:

23 SEPTEMBER

Therefore, as the Holy Spirit says, "Today, when you hear his voice..."

—Hebrews 3:7, RSV

The word, "today," rings with an immediacy and an imminence that I cannot escape. Today lies between two other days—yesterday, which is already dead, and tomorrow, which is waiting to be born. Today is all I really have, for I may not be here tomorrow—and I can do nothing about yesterday. Today vibrates with possibilities; it is loaded with potential; its treasures are incalculable. The curve of my life can be unalterably changed by what I do or leave undone today. The instant and far-reaching significance of even an hour cannot be exaggerated. Yet I must not let the practicalities of all this strain my soul. I must remember that leisure and relaxation are needed to balance my character. In this I follow the example of Jesus, who knew how to proportion his life, allowing leisure for friendship and relaxation to offset the pressures of ceaseless activity.

For further thought:
1. Does "today" have proper importance in my life?
2. Do I procrastinate—or take on too much?
3. What can I learn from Jesus?

Lord, help me today to:

And the Lord turned, and looked upon Peter. And Peter remembered the word of the Lord, how he said unto him, Before the cock crow, thou shalt deny me thrice. And Peter went out and wept bitterly.
—Luke 22:61, 62

Peter developed into the sturdy Christian he became because of a broken heart. Many times those around us who seem most serene and untroubled come to this acceptance of life by way of a broken heart. Some of the richest gifts of life are discovered only through profound and humbling sorrow. In the mystery of Christ's dealing with us, our cowardice, our untruthfulness, our selfish egotism, or any other sin once revealed to our conscience for what it really is, and truly repented of, becomes the occasion of new life for our souls through God's chastening grace. By repentance and forgiveness we may enter into a deeper spirituality, a more intimate communion with God, a stronger character for ourselves and a finer sympathy with others.

For further thought:
1. Do all come to Christ the way Peter did?
2. Does my life seem more serene than it really is?

Like Peter, Lord, I need to examine my life. Today I will:

25 SEPTEMBER

Read Psalm 119:97–112

How sweet are thy words to my taste, sweeter than honey to my mouth!
Through thy precepts I get understanding; I hate every false way.
—Psalm 119:103, 104, RSV

God speaks to the listening heart of the world in many voices. There has never been silence between the Infinite and the souls of men. But in the Bible there is gathered a collection of messages from the Spirit-filled men who have proved themselves the truest interpreters of God. The Word is "a lamp unto our feet and a light unto our path." It has come to us like a precious legacy from the past. We do not understand all of its wonderful meanings, but we discover in it even deeper springs of wisdom and life. Through the ages it discloses the truth to each generation. It endures while men and institutions pass.

Proof of the Bible's unique place in human life is not hard to find. We need only the simple trust to commit our souls to its teachings, and it will prove itself divine. May we study it to catch its spirit, to see how the men who have written down for us their messages and experiences upon its pages have spoken for God, to understand how through them God ever speaks to us. Most of all, may we see that the heart of the Book is Christ, the Light of the world.

For further thought:
1. Is the Bible "real" to me?
2. When I'm in a dark place, do I discover that the Word is a light to my path and a lamp to my feet?

With your Word as my guide today, Lord, I will:

For examples of patience in suffering, look at the Lord's prophets.
—James 5:10, LB

Suffering is not a popular subject—but it is an eye-opener. In our affluent, gadget-ridden day, we have lost sight of the pain and hardships suffered by the saints of yesteryear. They seem remote and almost legendary. But we forget that suffering is rampant in our world today as well—the persecution of the people of God is a reality, even though we often aren't aware of it. No life that has not known suffering is really complete; no culture that does not grow through severe discipline is mature. Most of us live in insulation, our lives seldom touched by sorrow or grief. But some of those around us live their lives surrounded by sorrow—and "acquainted with grief." We must be sensitive to their needs and remember with Leo Tolstoy that "it is by those who have suffered that the world has been advanced."

For further thought:
1. When I remember that Jesus was the "Suffering Servant," what does that do to my attitude toward suffering?
2. Is there such a thing as a "constructive suffering"?

Lord, help me to see suffering in proper perspective today as I:

Whatever happens, conduct yourselves in a manner worthy of the gospel of Christ. Then, whether I come and see you or only hear about you, I will know that you stand firm in one spirit, contending as one man for the faith of the gospel without being frightened in any way by those who oppose you....

—Philippians 1:27, 28, NIV

The mental picture one gets from this striking passage is that of a group of soldiers standing shoulder to shoulder either to protect their flank or to launch an effective offense. We Christians aren't called upon to be instant heroes, but we are called upon to be "instant in season, out of season" (2 Tim. 4:2). This demands consecration to the common tasks as well as to the crisis moments. These may arise out of ordinary circumstances—or they may rush in upon us from outside influences. Either way, our "strong purpose" unites us to face whatever comes in the strength God gives. It reminds me of John Wesley's comment in a letter to his brother, Charles: "I desire to have both heaven and hell ever in my eye, while I stand in this isthmus of life, between two boundless oceans."

For further reflection:
1. What does a verse like "Watch ye, stand fast in the faith, quit you like men; be strong" (1 Cor. 16:13) conjure up for me?
2. In what ways does a Christian soldier differ from an ordinary soldier?

As a Christian soldier, today I will:

There is nothing better for a man than that he should eat and drink, and find enjoyment in his toil. This also, I saw, is from the hand of God.

—Ecclesiastes 2:24, RSV

At first glance, this looks like a pretty shallow solution to the so-called mystery of life. For the Christian, there's a deeper dimension. For him, joy is not alone a blessing and a gift; it is also a duty and a virtue. Some lives are so orderly and filled with good health or inspiration or success that surface joy seems to spring up spontaneously. Others, however, must find joy in spite of illness, drab surroundings, dull routines, or hopeless defeats. Yet through the practice of prayer and the presence of Christ, those who seem least favored by circumstances somehow find the springs of true joy and drink from them despite outward drought. They respond with praise and thanksgiving to the pain and stress surrounding them.

For further thought:
1. What is the secret of inner joy?
2. How can I meet stress with strength?

With your help today, Lord, I will:

And he carried me away in the spirit to a great and high mountain, and showed me that great city, the holy Jerusalem, descending out of heaven from God.

—Revelation 21:10

It is common in our day for men to strive to improve the quality of life in our cities. Some dedicate themselves wholeheartedly and singlemindedly to such a task. It's a commendable goal, but not very realistic. Any hope for improving our environment must depend on the intervention and overruling hand of God. The Lord came to John as the apostle waited on the Isle of Patmos, and brought him a vision of a city that would be built in the skies and then let down to abide forever on the earth. This vision was simply God's way of saying to him and to us that the Holy City toward which our blundering human efforts tend is already a reality in the mind of God—and that its realization upon the earth will not come as the result of our toil but of God's intervention into the flow of history.

For further reflection:
1. What can I do to improve the quality of life around me?
2. What can I do to prepare for the coming King who is the only answer to the world's desperate need?

Lord, in preparation for your coming, today I will:

. . . Be thou faithful until death and I will give thee a crown of life. He that hath an ear, let him hear what the Spirit saith unto the churches; He that overcometh shall not be hurt of the second death.
—Revelation 2:10

J. R. Miller is one of my favorite devotional writers. Even though he died in 1912, his spiritual insight is applicable in any century. On the subject of faithfulness he says: "Men do not fly up mountains; they go up slowly, step by step. True Christian life is always mountain climbing—heaven is above us and ever keeps above us. It never gets easy to go heavenward. It is a slow and painful process to grow better. No one leaps to sainthood at a bound. No one gets the victory once and for all over his faults and sins. It is a struggle of years and every day must have its victories if we are ever to be final and complete overcomers. Yet while we cannot expect to reach the radiant mountaintop at one bound, we certainly ought to be climbing it step by step. We ought not to sit on the same little terrace, part way up the mountain, day by day. Higher and higher should be our unresting aim." That's a good motto for me to live by today!

For further reflection:
1. What kind of "faith" mountain am I climbing today?
2. What "faith" goals am I striving for?

Lord, today I will:

1 OCTOBER

Read Matthew 8:23–27

And he said to them, "Why are you afraid, O men of little faith?" Then he rose and rebuked the winds and the sea; and there was a great calm.

—Matthew 8:26, RSV

As I read this verse, I can't help but wonder if Jesus might not say this to me about my faith. I've been a Christian for many years, but I must confess that sometimes my faith is too small and willfully immature. More than once I've felt rebuked as I have seen the faith of a younger fellow Christian expressed in the wake of my own lack of faith. Not only do I limit God by my lack of faith; I'm convinced I must sometimes disappoint him as well. The secret of spiritual growth lies in a *Christ*-centered rather than an I-centered faith. In him I can do all things, Paul says. Without him, I stumble and fall, afraid to move forward, unable to function because of fear.

For further reflection:
1. If Jesus were to describe my faith, what word or words would he use?
2. What is the ultimate source of my faith?

With renewed faith, Lord, today I will:

Then Jesus went with them to a place called Gethsemane, and he said to his disciples, "Sit here, while I go yonder and pray."
—Matthew 26:36, RSV

Jesus took his chosen friends with him into Gethsemane. Those who love us most truly must share our sorrow with us. But it is noteworthy, also, that Jesus himself went deeper into the shadows of the garden than he asked his friends to go. Is not this fact most suggestive? We need not fear that in any grief of ours we shall ever be alone, without companionship. We shall never find ourselves in shadows too deep for the sympathy and help of the Christ. However far into the garden of sorrow we may ever be led, if we lift up our eyes we shall see that Jesus is on before us, a stone's-cast further than he has asked us to go.

J. R. MILLER (1840–1912)

For further thought:
1. Do I really comprehend and appreciate the agony Jesus went through in Gethsemane for me?
2. What does it mean that Jesus "went deeper" into the garden than he expected his friends [me included] to go?

Because I know others who are grief-stricken, today I will:

3 OCTOBER

And when those hired about the eleventh hour came, each of them received a denarius. Now when the first came, they thought they would receive more; but each of them also received a denarius.
—Matthew 20:9, 10, RSV

Jesus often used stories to illustrate eternal truths. This was one of them—and the lesson it teaches has often been obscured by well-meaning interpreters. Jesus tells me here that the *length* of my Christian life is not the important thing—it is the *fact* of it! Those who worked in the vineyard all day received no higher wage than those who began when the day was almost over. This story is not an illustration of the merit of Christian service—it is a perfect picture of God's grace in action. In the light of this truth I'd better spend less time judging and more time "journeying" to tell others about my blessed Savior.

For further reflection:
1. Do I sometimes fall into the trap of thinking myself "farther along" spiritually than the new Christian who sits down the pew from me?
2. What happens to my "halo" in the light of this story?

Lord, help me to tell _____ about you. Today I will:

The sheep hear his voice, and he calls his own sheep by name and leads them out.

—John 10:3, RSV

A beautiful truth underlying the Christian life emerges in this verse. The immortal A. W. Tozer put it this way: "The footprint of the obedient sheep is always found within the larger footprint of the shepherd." One must know something about the uniqueness of the Jewish shepherd to appreciate the truth being enunciated here. This shepherd, unlike the "mass production shepherd" in the United States, knew each of his sheep *individually*. And he did not *drive* them; he *led* them. They literally followed in his footprints. The "Great Shepherd of the sheep" leads us—and surrounds us with his care besides! What a blessed thought!

For further thought:
1. Would a fuller realization of this truth make a difference in where I go?
2. Do I ever "stray" in my walk with Jesus?

In your steps today, Lord, I will:

Let love be genuine; hate what is evil, hold fast to what is good; love one another with brotherly affection; outdo one another in showing honor.

—Romans 12:9, 10, RSV

When we lay our lives at Christ's feet in consecration, and tell him that we want to serve him with them, he gives them back to us again, and bids us use them in serving his people, our fellow-men. In the humblest and the lowliest of those who bear Christ's image Christ himself comes to us. We do not know when he stands before us in a lowly one who needs our sympathy or our help. It would be a sad thing if we turned him away unfed from our doors some day, or neglected to visit him in his sickness. Let us not say we love Christ if we are not ready to serve those whom he sends us to be served.

J. R. MILLER (1840–1912)

For further meditation:
1. Are there those in my life right now whom I can serve for Jesus' sake?
2. If not, what can I do to open my life to others?

Lord, today I feel you are telling me to:

... that I may know him and the power of his resurrection....
—Philippians 3:10, RSV

Here and in Romans Paul calls out for an intimacy with Jesus that has no parallel. The martyred missionary, Jim Elliot, wrote: "O, the fullness, pleasure, sheer excitement of knowing God on earth. I care not if I ever raise my voice again for him if only I may love him, please him." At the early age of twenty-three, Elliot had learned the urgency of *knowing* Jesus. I, too, wish I *knew* Jesus better. He should have my deepest love and devotion. If my primary purpose were to know him better, what changes would that necessitate in my life? It is more important that I *love* him than that I *serve* him. It's safe to say that because—if my love was this total, then my service would reflect that surrender of self to the Lordship of Christ.

For further reflection:
1. Do I really "know Jesus"—or is mine just a "nodding acquaintance"?
2. If Paul's plea here was mine, what difference would that make in my life?

Lord, to know you better today I will:

To the thirsty I will give from the fountain of the water of life without payment.

—Revelation 21:6, RSV

The apostle John, writer of the Revelation, must have had an earlier scene in mind when he wrote these words. How reminiscent they are of Jesus' words to the Samaritan woman: "If you knew the gift of God, and who it is... saying to you, 'Give me a drink,' you would have asked him and he would have given you living water" (John 4:10, RSV). It's impossible to quench physical thirst permanently, but permanent quenching of spiritual thirst *is* possible at the fountain of Life himself—Jesus Christ. I've knelt to drink from a mountain stream, and in so doing pictured the humility which must be a part of quenching spiritual thirst. *Kneeling* to drink is a symbol of the surrender necessary if we are to truly slake our spiritual thirst. If I come in a haughty spirit to my Savior, I'll miss the great blessing of his living waters.

For further reflection:
1. How do I come to Jesus—proudly or humbly?
2. What bucket will he fill with living water—the empty one or the one filled with worldly concerns?

Today I turn my life over to you, Lord. Fill it with your living water and:

OCTOBER 8

Whosoever therefore shall confess me before men, him will I confess also before my Father which is in heaven.

—Matthew 10:32

What does it mean to "confess" the Lord Jesus! More recent translations (RSV, NAS, etc.) use the word "acknowledge" here. And that's really what "confession" is—to acknowledge or admit something as truth or fact. This may take the form of "witnessing," as it does when one testifies in court. In this case, I merely tell what I know—what I have seen or experienced. My *opinion* of what I saw or experienced is not admissible as evidence—but my unvarnished statement of what I saw or experienced is. The biblical concept of confession involves more than speech, however. I "confess" by the way I live as well. If I don't "practice what I preach," my spoken words won't mean much to those whose lives I touch. But I can know this for a certainty: If I outspokenly acknowledge Jesus Christ as my Savior and Lord, and *live* that witness as well, then Jesus will "acknowledge" me before his Father in heaven.

For further reflection:
1. Do I "confess" Jesus verbally?
2. Do my verbal witness and my lifestyle jibe?
3. If not, what do I need to change?

Lord, today help me to:

9 OCTOBER

Therefore I tell you, whatever you ask in prayer, believe that you have received it, and it will be yours.

—Mark 11:24, RSV

Christ never compels any one to take the gifts and blessings which he has to bestow. We complain of our sparse blessedness. We wonder why God does not manifest himself to us as he has done to others. We wonder why we cannot have such power in prayer as some Christians have—why so little seems to come from our work for Christ. It is not from any lack of power in Christ, for his strength never fails nor wastes; it is because we will not receive what he brings. Unbelief shuts up Christ's hand so that it cannot give to us the things of his grace, or cannot work deliverances for us. Thus our unbelief keeps us impoverished. It hides God's face, and robs us of the deep, rich joys which faith would bring. Shall we not pray for simple faith, that we may receive large things?

J. R. MILLER (1840–1912)

For further thought:

1. How does my "failure of faith" rob me of God's blessing?
2. What problems has my unbelief caused me and others recently?

In faith, today I will:

He who is faithful in a very little is faithful also in much; and he who is dishonest in a very little is dishonest also in much.

—Luke 16:10, RSV

Jesus' statement here reminds me of the person with only one talent who hides behind his limitations and says, "Since there is so little I can do, I'll simply sit here and do nothing." Such a one is succumbing to the temptation to be a "spectator" rather than a participant in the Christian life. On the other hand, the one with more than one talent is often the one who gives himself whole-heartedly to the work of the Lord. It is tragic that the "one talent" person thus often misses out on the thrill of the Christian life for want of participation in it. The Living Bible is even more specific and to the point: "*No!* For unless you are honest in small matters, you won't be in large ones. If you cheat even a little, you won't be honest with greater responsibilities. And if you are untrustworthy about worldly wealth, who will trust you with the true riches of heaven?" (vv. 10, 11).

For further reflection:
1. Where do I fit in this picture Jesus is painting?
2. Am I guilty of being a spectator when I should be a participant?
3. Is this a form of dishonesty as the Scriptures imply?

Lord, I want to use my abilities for you. Help me today to:

11 OCTOBER

Read Isaiah 43:1–7

When thou passest through the waters, I will be with thee; and through the rivers, they shall not overflow thee: when thou walkest through the fire, thou shalt not be burned.

—Isaiah 43:2

This promise does not tell us we shall not need to pass through deep water, nor does it say we shall not cross turbulent rivers, nor walk in the furnace of affliction. What it does say is that, though those things may come to us, we need not go through them alone. The Great I AM will go with us every step of the way. He measures the depth of the water, the swiftness of the river's current, the intensity of the furnace heat. And His love will not allow the water to be one fraction of an inch deeper than we can pass through. His compassion will not allow the river's current to be one mite stronger than we can stand. His goodness will control the temperature of the furnace so that it will only refine our gold.

OLIVER G. WILSON

For further consideration and thought:
1. Do I live in the consciousness of the biblical truth that I am not alone?
2. What can I consciously do to increase my awareness that God is indeed with me?

Lord, realizing your presence with me, today I will:

Take your share of suffering as a good soldier of Jesus Christ, just as I do.

—2 Timothy 2:3, LB

"A good soldier," it has been said, "both abstains and sustains." This is what it means to endure hardness. A good soldier has not only to fight in aggressive conflict; he has to withstand in defensive warfare. His power is seen far more in what he can *bear* than in what he can *do*. How applicable all this is spiritually! To be a good soldier of Jesus Christ, we must know the discipline of laying aside every encumbrance, every weight, every entanglement. By actual experience we must learn how to "refuse" as well as how to accept. We often lose as much by yielding to the allurements of the world as we do by failing to claim the provisions of grace. The "hardness" that is essential to being a "good soldier" can be brought about only by the discipline of trial, and loyalty to this law of the kingdom— that we "please him who hath chosen" us to be his soldiers. Character is formed by conduct, and good conduct is the outcome of a living faith in a personal Savior. In 1 Timothy 6:12 Paul tells his spiritual son, "Fight the good fight of faith."

For further thought:
1. Do I take my share of suffering as a good soldier—or do I complain and whine?
2. In the fight of faith, am I a "soldier" or a "sitter"?

As a "good soldier" today I will:

Walk in newness of life.

—Romans 6:4

Both life and liberty are needed before we are ready to "walk." This life is secured to us in Christ. He is our life. So too is liberty. Deliverance from sin's power, as well as from sin's penalty, is the fruit of Christ's death. "Stand fast therefore in the liberty wherewith *Christ hath made us free*" (Gal. 5:1, italics mine). We are set free, not for idle contemplation or personal enjoyment, but for practical service. Walking in newness of life involves the whole of that life which glorifies God. It is Paul's favorite term for moral conduct. He says "newness of life," instead of "new life," because he wants to emphasize the idea of the new nature dominating this second life. The old life terminates at the cross. If we died with Christ, then the life that belongs to the "man of old" has been brought to an end. And if we are risen with Christ, we have entered into the life of the "new man." That is a life of freedom and of power. Walking in this life is not a hard, irksome struggle, but free and joyous action. What physical exercise is to the man who is in robust health, "walking in newness of life" is to the one who is living in the power of Christ's resurrection.

For further thought:
1. When does this "newness of life" take effect?
2. In what ways does physical exercise parallel spiritual exercise?

As part of my "walk" today, I will:

I pray not that thou shouldest take them out of the world, but that thou shouldest keep them from the evil.

—John 17:15

I have sometimes wondered why the Lord should leave his children here on planet earth, when he could have saved them from so many dangers and snares by taking them out of the world. It might seem logical to my human mind that he should immediately remove us from scenes of such painful conflict and alluring temptations. But our Lord has a gracious purpose in keeping his people for a season still in the world. "I pray not that thou shouldest take them out of the world." What would the world do without Christ's witnesses on the earth? I pray, the Lord says, "that thou shouldest keep them from the evil," and emphatically from the *Evil One*. It is he who is behind all temptations, who is the worker in every subtle plot. "That *thou* shouldest keep them" (italics mine). Blessed is the man who is thus divinely kept. We cannot keep ourselves. "The *Lord* is thy Keeper" (Ps. 121:5, italics mine). How slow some of us are to learn that fact! This is the privilege of every blood-bought soul—to be "kept by the power of God through faith unto salvation."

For further thought:
1. Do I live my life conscious of God's "keeping" power?
2. Have I experienced his "keeping" in recent days?
3. Do I ever consider what "might have been" if God had *not* been keeping me?

As one of Christ's witnesses, today I will:

So Jesus had compassion on them, and touched their eyes; and immediately their eyes received sight, and they followed him.

—Matthew 20:34

Christ no longer goes about in person among men, laying his hands on the sick, the lame, the blind, the children. This work he has entrusted to his disciples. He wants us to represent him. He wants us to be to the sick, the sorrowing, the stricken, the fallen, what he would be to them if he were here again on the earth. It is not hard for us to know, therefore, what it is to be a true Christian. We have but to study the story of our Lord's life, watching how he helped and blessed others, to get the key to all Christian duty. His miracles we cannot repeat, but his sympathy, his gentleness, his thoughtfulness, his unselfishness, are patterns for our human imitation. If we catch his inner spirit, "the mind that was in Christ," we will become great blessings wherever we go in his name. Then our touch will soothe, our words will comfort, strengthen, and inspire, and our deeds of love will leave benedictions on every life.

J. R. MILLER (1840–1912)

For further consideration:
1. Do I faithfully carry out my mission as a disciple?
2. To whom should I especially "represent" Christ at this time in my life?

In the light of this meditation, today I will:

He hath prepared for them a city.

—Hebrews 11:16

"A city" is just one of the many things which we are told God has prepared for his people. The gospel is spoken of under the figure of a feast ready for the guests: "I have *prepared* my dinner" (Matt. 22:4, italics mine). To those who enter into his glory he says, "Inherit the kingdom *prepared* for you from the foundation of the world" (Matt. 25:34, italics mine).

Then we read, "Eye hath not seen, nor ear heard, neither have entered into the heart of man, the things which God hath *prepared* for them that love him. But God hath revealed them unto us by his Spirit" (1 Cor. 2:9, 10, italics mine).

And so, in connection with our daily walk, how wonderful it is to learn that we have been "created in Christ Jesus for good works, which God *prepared* beforehand, that we should walk in them" (Eph. 2:10, RSV).

In whichever direction we look, we find that God's wisdom, and love, and power have been exercised on our behalf. In the past, the atoning sacrifice has been "prepared." In the future, our habitation in heaven has been prepared. "He hath prepared for them a city."

For further thought:

1. Why does the writer to the Hebrews use the term "city" to denote a place of blessing?
2. What are some of the characteristics of this "city" God has prepared?

Looking forward to this "city" prepared for me, today I will:

The Lord God omnipotent reigneth.

—Revelation 19:6

The believer in the process of being "tried" often has to remind himself that the God of his salvation is the Lord omnipotent. Without giving way to open unbelief, it is sometimes a temptation to yield to the habit of limiting God's grace and power. This was the sin of God's redeemed people of old. The psalmist says: "They . . . limited the Holy One of Israel" (Ps. 78:41). That is, they placed a limit on God's power. They said he could do this, and that—but could he spread a table in the wilderness? This was as much as to say that God was not omnipotent, and to deny his omnipotence was to deny his deity. This then was Israel's sin. How often we modern children of God are guilty of the same sin of limiting God! We need always to keep before us this divine attribute—"The Lord God omnipotent reigneth." He is Almighty to save, and to keep. He says: "All power is given unto me in heaven. and in earth" (Matt. 28:18). David says: "Some trust in chariots, and some in horses: but we will remember the name of the Lord our God" (Ps. 20:7). That is, we will remember who he is, and what he is. A perspective on his attributes will calm our fears and deliver us from the sin of unbelief (see Ps. 9:10; Luke 18:27).

For further thought:
1. Do I truly live as though the Lord were reigning in my world?
2. What would I do differently if I lived this way?

If the Lord really reigned in my life, today I would:

Whoso trusteth in the Lord, happy is he.

—Proverbs 16:20

We never know the meaning of trust until we learn the nature of trial. It is in trial that we have to put into practice the theory of believing in God. Trust is to become the habit of the soul. But often I am perplexed about faith, because, instead of being occupied with the Object of faith, I am thinking of the act of believing. But faith never comes in this way. It has no existence apart from him who is the object of it. "Whoso trusteth *in the Lord.*" Let our thoughts be occupied with God's revealed character, with what he is to us and what he has done for us, and we shall, without trying to believe, begin to put our trust in him. It is with what God is that I must be occupied; my mind then finds its resting place in God, and I know a peace that could never be found in the world. I see then how true are the words, "Happy is he."

Trial therefore is the testing ground or school for trust. It is there I learn the lesson of implicitly confiding in God, and of waiting patiently on him.

For further meditation:
1. Has my faith in God's ability to care for me been growing lately?
2. What recent experiences have been growing times for me?

Today I will show my trust by:

Humble yourselves therefore under the mighty hand of God, that he may exalt you in due time.

—1 Peter 5:6

Properly understood, these words teach us the secret of humility. How to be humble is the question that often plagues us. We see its necessity; we admire the grace of humility in others; we want to be humble ourselves. But how do we make it happen? A power greater than our own is needed; it must be the power of God. Peter says that the secret of humility lies in "the mighty hand of God." And how shall we get the benefit of that power? We must yield to it. In other words, we must get "under" it. Just as we may become partakers of the power of evil by yielding to it, so it is by yielding to the power of God that we partake of his power and produce good rather than evil. It is not by struggling or striving to make ourselves humble that we attain the grace of humility. We must cease from self, and submit to the power of God. The power that alone can bring us to the dust, and keep us there, resides in God, and not in us. We humble ourselves under his hand when we are willing to take his will instead of our own—when we accept his leading instead of trying to go it on our own.

For further thought:
1. Is it my policy and practice to yield—or struggle?
2. Am I more interested in learning humility—or do I desire to be exalted?

Lord, today let me learn:

I am cast out of thy sight; yet I will look again toward thy holy temple.
—Jonah 2:4

An erroneous idea of God is a serious hindrance to prayer. Jonah, though he was aware of God's existence and believed in his power, needed to learn much about his love and his grace. The purpose of all God's dealings with us is to bring us to himself—to bring us to him in prayer; to teach us to approach him with a true spirit of loving confidence. Though we have a saving knowledge of God, there may yet be much misconception as to his true character. Sometimes we may fall into error by thinking of him as less loving, less merciful, less gracious than he is. We may look at him through the atmosphere of adverse circumstances and interpret him by what we see and feel. This is not the way of faith. Then it is we are tempted to say, "I am cast out of thy sight." But when we regard him by the way of faith, then we learn to interpret circumstances by what God is, as he has revealed himself to us through his Word, and in his Son Jesus Christ. Here we have the secret of true liberty and power in prayer.

For further thought:
1. Is my view of who God is sometimes obscured by my circumstances?
2. Am I ever like Jonah in my perception of God and my rebellion against him?

Lord, my prayer today is:

21 OCTOBER

That ye might walk worthy of the Lord unto all pleasing, being fruitful in every good work, and increasing in the knowledge of God.
—Colossians 1:10

To be fruitful in the sense of being involved in "every good work" is one thing, and to be fruitful in every good work that we are engaged in is another. In the first sense the multiplicity of good works is the thought before us—in the other, the fruitfulness of our lives is the thing emphasized. I may be busy in a number of good works, and fruitful in none of them. If I am perpetually giving way to irritability, to anxious worry, to pride, to harsh judgments and evil-speaking, however active and busy I may be in all these good works, I will not be "fruitful" in them. Fruit is not the outcome of outward action, but of the inner life. Fruit is the result of the Holy Spirit's indwelling—of his gracious, unhindered activity within us. It is not the result of human energy, nor is it the product of the Spirit's power apart from the cooperation of our wills and affections. We yield ourselves to him, and he takes full possession of our whole beings, and brings every power and faculty of our renewed nature into contribution to this end, that we should bear much fruit.

For further thought:
1. Am I concerned about being fruitful for God?
2. What do I need to do to correct my perspective of fruitfulness?

The "good work" I should be involved in now is:

No man has ever seen God; if we love one another, God abides in us and his love is perfected in us.

—1 John 4:12, RSV

We ought not to need night to teach us the glories of the day. We ought not to have to wait for sorrow before we can appreciate the sweetness of joy. Yet is it not often true that we learn the value of our blessings but by their loss? Many a time an empty chair is the first full revealer of the worth and faithfulness of a precious human friendship. Would it not be well if we were to seek to appreciate our good things while we have them? We would then have the joy itself, and not merely the dull pain of regret as we look back at blessings vanished. Besides, we would do more for our friends while they are with us if we appreciated their worth. Too many of us never understand what we owe to our dear ones until there remains no further opportunity of paying love's debt.

J. R. MILLER (1840–1912)

For further thought:
1. Is there someone in my life whom I am taking for granted?
2. Is there someone in my life whose absence would finally make me appreciate him or her?

Today I will show appreciation for:

23 OCTOBER

By their fruits ye shall know them.

—Matthew 7:20

There are three things in the Christian life that should be distinguished—fruit, gifts, and works. A man may be busy in Christian work without abounding in fruit. Fruit is something higher and more spiritual than works. It grows out of the influence and the infilling of the divine life in the soul. The fruit of the Spirit is absent in the life of the man who is habitually grieving the Holy Spirit, however active in work or zealous in doctrine he may be. We have to be *fruitful in every good work* (see Col 1:10). It is not by their works ye shall know them, but by their *fruits*.

Then, again, I must remember fruit and gifts are not to be confused. A man may be gifted as a preacher or teacher of the Word, but he can be nevertheless lacking in the fruit of the Spirit. Those "gifts" may draw crowds, and hundreds may be brought to Christ through the Word preached, and yet if we judged the man's true spiritual condition by his "gifts," we would come to a wrong conclusion. "By their *fruits* ye shall know them." Let there be genuine humility, an ignoring of self, and you have then "fruit," which is distinct from "works" and from "gifts."

For further meditation:

1. Am I a fruit-bearing Christian?
2. As I meditate on the list of fruit given in Galatians 5:22, 23, do I see evidence of them in my life?

I think the most obvious "fruit" in my life is:

The king of Israel, even the Lord, is in the midst of thee: thou shalt not see evil any more.

—Zephaniah 3:15

This fact is repeated in the seventeenth verse with some additions. "The Lord thy God in the midst of thee is mighty." Two facts are there stated: *what* he is, and *where* he is. He is the Lord *thy* God. This implies a covenant relationship with him. He is mighty. And this mighty One takes up his abode in the midst of his people—and in the heart of each believer. All things are therefore possible to him who is thus possessed. The Lord himself dwells in his children to save and to keep.

Can we say that we have thus enthroned him in our hearts? The Holy Spirit strengthens us to this end, that Christ may dwell in our hearts by faith (Eph. 3:17). In this way he takes up permanent residence in our lives. Thus enthroned he controls our whole being, and transforms the outer person as well as the inner experience. "I will save" (Zeph. 19). That refers to a daily and continuous salvation—an ongoing deliverance from sin's power and service. It is in this salvation that we find the fullest joy, because we are being preserved blameless, and kept continually in the light of God's countenance.

For further thought:
1. Am I seated on the throne of my heart and life—or is God?
2. What does it mean to let God have full control of my life?

Lord, today I yield the following areas of my life to you:

25 OCTOBER

Be strong in the grace that is in Christ Jesus.

—2 Timothy 2:1

What is the source of the strength with which we are to be empowered? It is in Christ Jesus. In no sense is it in ourselves. Power is not given to us as something to be used independently of him. It is *divine power*, both as to its exercise and its source. Then, again, we are not called upon here to strengthen ourselves, but rather to *allow* ourselves to *be* strengthened. The verb is in the passive voice. "Be strong—strengthened inwardly—in the grace (spiritual blessing) that is [to be found only] in Christ Jesus" (AB).

It is the function of the Holy Spirit to strengthen us. He does this by bringing us into the center and source of all power. It pleased the father that all fulness of grace should dwell in Jesus Christ. It is to him that the Spirit leads us. It is of the things of Christ that the Spirit takes and reveals unto us (John 16:14). And it is his might that the Spirit communicates to us. But as we said, we do not receive strength apart from him, but in union and communion with him. Paul elsewhere describes it as being "strengthened with all might, according to his glorious power" (Col. 1:11). When we are thus strengthened, we have no consciousness of strength in ourselves. It is then that we know our own weakness. But we have the power of Christ.

For further thought:
1. From where do I draw my strength?
2. To whom do I habitually look for strength?

Lord, in the strength you give today I will:

Having loved his own which were in the world, he loved them unto the end.

—John 13:1

This passage makes clear the distinction between Christ's people and the world. His people are the objects of his special love; he regards them as "his own." They are his peculiar treasure. For a time he has them left in the world, and yet they are not of it. They are placed there to serve and represent him. His love for them is unchanging. He loves them to the end—to the uttermost. What he did for his disciples at this time was deeply significant. It represented what he would do for his people throughout time. In lowly humility he washed their feet. So great is his love to us, that he is still doing this for his disciples now. Our most humble walk, or holiest obedience, needs his continual washing. We are *his*. He has bought us with his own blood. He has loved us with an everlasting love. His grace has triumphed over us, so that we are his, not by purchase only, but by power—renewing and transforming power. And the love that constrained him when he died to redeem us is the same love that goes out every day to renew and to cleanse, to transform and to keep, until we shall appear with him in glory.

For further thought:
1. Am I living in an awareness of Christ's love?
2. What does "he loved them unto the end" mean?

In the light of your love, Lord, today I will:

27 OCTOBER

We look not at the things which are seen ... for the things which are seen are temporal; but the things which are not seen are eternal.
—2 Corinthians 4:18

From the context we see that the main thought of the passage is the spiritual transformation of our character. The outward man is perishing or dying—the inward man is daily being renewed. This process should go on continually. But it is conditional. It goes on "while we are looking not at the things which are seen, but at the things which are not seen"; in other words, it is while we are living and walking by faith—while we continue to see him who is invisible to the unbeliever.

The believer lives in two worlds at once. There is the outward world of sense. Of course the believer is extremely aware of the things that are seen. And there is the invisible world of faith. The unseen is as real as the seen—in fact, more so, because the things which are seen are temporal, and the things which are not seen are eternal. It is the unseen world that is the true and the real—the visible is but the shadow. As Christians we are two dimensional—living in the best of both worlds, as it were.

As we live surrounded by the things that are seen, let us not look *at* them, but *beyond* them.

For further thought:
1. Which world is most real to me—the temporal material world, or the unseen and eternal dimension?
2. In which world do I expect to spend the most time?

In the light of eternity, today I will:

When the day of Pentecost had come, they were all together in one place. And suddenly a sound came from heaven like the rush of a mighty wind, and it filled all the house where they were sitting.
—Acts 2:1, 2, RSV

I would love to have been one of the company of believers as the Holy Spirit came upon his people the first time. What a moving moment this must have been! Yet, if I only stop and think about it, his coming on his people can be and is just as dramatic and full of impact today. My problem probably is that I'm so wrapped up in the everyday effort to "make it" that I don't sense his tug at my sleeve or touch on my shoulder. I'm the loser because I'm too wrapped up in the mundane and the mercenary to feel the presence of the Eternal.

For further thought:
1. What spiritual blessing have I missed (today or yesterday) because I haven't taken time to sense the Spirit?
2. What in my life hinders the Spirit's ministry to me?

Lord, help me today to empty my life and make room for your Holy Spirit. Today, I will:

29 OCTOBER

When God created man, he made him in the likeness of God.
—Genesis 5:1, RSV

This is a clear-cut statement of fact—a forthright and factual pronouncement of a tremendous truth. Over the last one hundred years or so the intellectual community has sought to prove God a liar and man a product of evolution by attacking the concept of creation. But God's blessed birth announcement of man's divine origin stands amid the wreckage of the many man-made theories that have been expressed concerning man's roots. Interestingly enough, the New Testament affirms what the Old Testament states. For example, John writes: "Beloved, now are we the sons of God, and it doth not yet appear what we shall be: but we know that, when he shall appear, we shall be like him; for we shall see him as he is" (1 John 3:2). Rational man's attacks do not shake our foundation as the product of the Creator's hand.

For further thought:
1. In light of this tremendous fact, how and for whom should I live my life?
2. What does my recognition that I am "in the likeness of God" do for my self-image?

Lord, as one made in your likeness, today I will:

Behold, I have set the land before you; go in and take possession of the land which the Lord swore to your fathers, to Abraham, to Isaac, and to Jacob, to give to them and to their descendants after them.
—Deuteronomy 1:8, RSV

This verse echoes the command of God to Abraham, "Arise, walk through the length and the breadth of the land, for I will give it to you" (Gen. 13:17, RSV). When God lays a prayer burden on my heart, it's because he wants me to move forward and "take possession of the land." When I'm faced with an important decision, he has "set the land before" me and wants me to move ahead into it. Not only my prayer burdens and decisions come under his care, but also the opportunities to witness and work for him. The people I work with or who cross my path in the midst of my day—they are placed there as part of the land I'm to possess.

For further reflection:
1. What is my prayer burden today?
2. What is my crucial decision today?
3. What is my witnessing opportunity today?

Lord, today help me to "possess":

31 OCTOBER

Flee for your life; do not look back or stop... flee to the hills, lest you be consumed.

—Genesis 19:17, RSV

One of the temptations of the human condition is to "look back." Jesus was recognizing that principle when he said, "No one who puts his hand to the plow and looks back is fit for the kingdom of God" (Luke 9:62, RSV). How do I handle this tendency to look back? Simply by making it my practice to "look up"! The upward look is the best antidote for the backward look. The psalmist once said, "I will lift up my eyes to the mountains; From whence shall my help come? My help comes from the Lord . . ." (Ps. 121:1, 2, NAS). In Psalm 123 he repeated, "to Thee I lift up my eyes" (v. 1, NAS). I shouldn't fall for the temptation to look back. Instead I should be practicing the upward look.

For further thought:
1. Where do I habitually look?
2. If I usually look back, what can I do to change that habit?

Looking *up* to you, Lord, today I will:

NOVEMBER 1

... When God destroyed the cities of the valley, God remembered Abraham. ...

—Genesis 19:29, RSV

The moral condition of the "cities of the valley," Sodom and Gomorrah, is reminiscent of that which prevailed in the whole world of Noah's day—and disturbingly like conditions in our own day. But in the midst of the godlessness and wickedness, "God remembered Abraham," his chosen child. And he remembers me, his child today as well. Just as surely as he promised to reward wickedness with punishment, he promises good to his children: "... They that seek the Lord shall not want any good thing" (Ps. 34:10.) The same God who said, "Be sure your sins will find you out," loved the world so much that he gave his only begotten Son, that "whosoever believeth in him should not perish, but have everlasting life" (John 3:16).

For further consideration:
1. What is the general direction of my life—toward evil or toward good?
2. Is my life making any impact for good on the world around me?

Lord, help me today to:

Now the earth was corrupt in God's sight, and the earth was filled with violence. And God saw the earth, and behold, it was corrupt; for all flesh had corrupted their way upon the earth.

—Genesis 6:11–12, RSV

Reading this description of the earth in Noah's day reminds me of the world in which I live. Physicist Albert Einstein (1879–1955) said of the human condition, "The real problem is in the hearts and minds of men. It is not a problem of physics but of ethics. It is easier to denature plutonium than to denature the evil spirit of man." It was the evil in the hearts of men in Noah's day that caused the chaos—and it is the same root of evil that creates our current condition. But just as Noah found favor in God's sight, we Christians should do the same. Our lives should reflect the Christlike and the ethical. Our good conduct should stand out against the dark backdrop of the evil around us.

For further reflection:
1. Is there any difference between me and the world around me?
2. If I were imprisoned for being a Christian, would there be enough evidence to convict me?

As I look at the world around me, Lord, I feel I should:

NOVEMBER 3

And Abraham stretched forth his hand, and took the knife to slay his son.

—Genesis 22:10

Abraham is a fascinating character, truly a giant in God's hall of fame. And this pivotal passage from his story teaches a striking truth about obedience: it's not negotiable. If Abraham had not picked up the knife and started to plunge it into his son's heart, his obedience would have only been partial. And there's no such thing as *partial* obedience. Just as one cannot be neutral in his attitude toward Jesus Christ—neither for nor against—one cannot go only part way down the path toward obedience. It's all or nothing! Abraham had waited a lifetime for the "son of promise." It must have mystified him when God told him to sacrifice his beloved son (Gen. 22:2). But he was ready to do it, unanswered questions or not.

For further reflection:
1. What would I have done in Abraham's place?
2. Is God asking me to place some "beloved son" on the altar?

Lord, today I give you:

4 NOVEMBER

... I being in the way, the Lord led me....
—Genesis 24:27

God's guidance is conditional. The experience recorded here, of Abraham's servant, is a perfect example of that fact. And the condition is obedience. The servant was *"in* the way" when he experienced a wonderful sense of God's guidance. Another translation has it *"on* the way" (MLB). If I'm expecting God to guide me, I must be *"on* the way." I must be willing to step out in faith, believing that God will go before me and work out every detail in my path. In a sense, this is also an illustration of what conversion is. It's a turning about and moving into the way God would have me go, and it's a willingness to allow him to lead me in that way. I cannot expect God's guidance if I am not already in his way.

For further reflection:
1. Am I willing to be willing?
2. Am I aware of God's leading in my life?
3. Is there an area of disobedience in my life?

Lord, today I want to turn the following area of my life over to you:

He [Jehoshaphat] joined him [Ahaziah] in building ships.... And the ships were wrecked and were not able to go to Tarshish.
—2 Chronicles 20:36, 37, RSV

In Jehoshaphat's day, as in ours, there was a school of thought that said, "Anything goes in business!" Jehoshaphat's partnership with Ahaziah was purely a business deal. It was commercially right but morally wrong. In associating himself with the evil Ahaziah, Jehoshaphat descended to the moral level of his partner. And despite the overall upward trend of Jehoshaphat's reign, this venture ended in shipwreck. That shipwreck is a lesson for every Christian: We are to draw the line. Our lives from Monday through Saturday are to bear witness to what we profess on Sunday. When Solomon went into the merchant marine business, everything went well with him because his association did not compromise his principles. Purity of purpose is the only way to go!

For further thought:
1. Am I compromising my principles in any associations?
2. Do I have an Ahaziah in my background?

Lord, today I will:

6 NOVEMBER

He gives power to the faint, and to him who has no might he increases strength. Even youths shall faint and be weary, and young men shall fall exhausted; but they who wait for the Lord shall renew their strength....

—Isaiah 40:29–31, RSV

There are two ways to serve God. Unfortunately, most of us attempt to follow the first route, *physical energy,* and wear ourselves out in the process. We wind up like David in Psalm 22: "My strength is dried up like a potsherd, and my tongue cleaves to my jaws" (v. 15, RSV). That's a pretty graphic description of the physical exhaustion we can experience as we try to serve God in our own strength. The other way is to use *the energy of God!* Isaiah says that "they who wait for the Lord shall renew their strength.... they shall run and not be weary, they shall walk and not faint." The older I get, the more firmly I am impressed with this truth. There's a seldom quoted verse in which Zechariah puts it another way: "it will be a unique day known [only] to the Lord... but at evening there will be light" (14:7, MLB). God doesn't mean an unusually bright *twilight*—he means a brand new *sunrise!* An old Puritan once said to a tired Christian with too many irons in the fire, "Something's wrong, friend. Nothing is so refreshing as life for God in the power of the Spirit." I need to cry out for the filling of God's Spirit, when I'm faced with tiring tasks. *I* might get tired but *God* doesn't (Isa. 40:38)!

For further reflection:
1. Am I truly trying to serve God?
2. If so, in whose strength am I serving?

Lord, I really want to serve you in your strength. Today I will:

Then Peter, filled with the Holy Spirit.... When they saw the bold-ness of Peter and John, and perceived that they were uneducated, common men, they wondered; and they recognized that they had been with Jesus.

—Acts 4:8, 13, RSV

Peter and John may have been "uneducated, common men"—but they were powerful servants under the mighty hand of God. He is never frustrated by our superficial limitations, and a seeming shortage in the area of education is just that—superficial. If the world's wisdom were the criterion of Christian service, Jesus would have set up his disciple-recruiting booth outside Jerusalem University, but instead he went onto the "highways and byways" for his followers. If I base my hopes for usefulness in Christian service on climbing an academic ladder, I'll be disappointed to find that the ladder leans on nothing but empty air. This is not to disparage higher education as preparation for Christian service; it is simply an encouragement to those of us who may not have had the opportunity for such improvement. Knowing God intimately is the best qualification for Christian service. An adequate experience of Christ—being "filled with the Holy Spirit"—is the best degree of dedication. Of Peter and John it was said, "They recognized that they had been with Jesus." That's the place for preparation for Christian service.

For further thought:
1. Do I impress people with my credentials—or my commitment?
2. Peter and John were "uneducated, common men," but Paul was one of the best-educated men of his day. What does this tell me about effective Christian service?

Lord, today I will:

8 NOVEMBER

"And now, Lord, look upon their threats, and grant to thy servants to speak thy word with all boldness."... And when they had prayed, the place in which they were gathered together was shaken; and they were all filled with the Holy Spirit and spoke the word of God with boldness.

—Acts 4:29, 31, RSV

This episode, while not an account of the Holy Spirit's initial coming at Pentecost, certainly reads like the events of that exciting time. The disciples prayed for *boldness*, and in the face of this crisis situation they received just that. Filled with the Holy Spirit, they made an impact on those around them as great as what transpired on the day of Pentecost. It wouldn't be proper to describe this as a *second* Pentecost, for one was all that was needed to launch this church age. But it does illustrate a truth I need to remember: one filling is not enough. I need a fresh infilling of the Spirit for the new challenges that face me, just as these early Christians did. They had been present at Pentecost only a few months before, but that infilling was not sufficient for the new situation. Dwight L. Moody once said, "If the Spirit comes upon us afresh, I have no doubt about success. But if we are cold and indifferent, then our work will be superficial. It will not be lasting. If God calls us to a work, he can qualify us to do it." With the hymn writer I sing, "Spirit of the living God, fall fresh on me!"

For further reflection:
1. What kind of boldness do I have in the spiritual realm?
2. In what areas am I bolder? Why?

Lord, my prayer today is:

*Seven sons of a Jewish high priest named Sceva were doing this....
And the man in whom the evil spirit was leaped on them, mastered all
of them, and overpowered them, so that they fled out of that house
naked and wounded.*

—Acts 19:14, 16, RSV

I'm convinced that God has a sense of humor—or at least Luke,
the author of Acts, does. He graphically recounts this scene of the
seven sons of Sceva rushing pell-mell from their house like a nudist
colony running from a forest fire. This whole episode is a classic
biblical picture of trying to do the *endeavors* of God without first
receiving the *endowment* of God. Impressed with Paul's Spirit-filled
performance, the seven tried to put on a show of their own. They
were sure it would be simple: find a man possessed by demons, set
him up in front of the people, shout "Jesus! Jesus! Jesus!" a few
times—and rake in the receipts. They had reckoned without the
demon in the man, for he sneered, "Jesus I know, and Paul I
know—but who are you?" Am I like these sons of Sceva—trying to
do God's work in my own strength? Those seven young men were
sons of the high priest, by all earthly criteria well-suited for altar
service, but they did not have the Spirit's empowering. O God, help
me not to make the same mistake!

For further reflection:
1. Do I come back to the "filling station" before trying to do
   exploits for God?
2. In what ways can I experience this infilling?

Lord, fill me today, and help me to:

But Jacob said to him, "My Lord knows that the children are frail and that the flocks and herds giving suck are a care to me; and if they are overdriven for one day, all the flocks will die. Let my lord pass on before his servant, and I will lead on slowly, according to the pace of the cattle which are before me and according to the pace of the children...."

—Genesis 33:13, 14, RSV

A new Jacob emerges here. When God changed Jacob's name (see Gen. 32:28), he also changed his nature. Hasty Jacob is now a new man—a slower man. In fact, the King James Version uses the descriptive term, "lead on *softly,* according as the... children be able to endure" (italics mine). Jacob, the "supplanter," is now Israel, "the prince with God," who treats his family with love and caring. The one who used to *leap* ahead impetuously now limps slowly, consideration for others his primary concern. This was the result of a night spent in prayer—a man transformed from selfishness to selflessness. Only the entrance of the Holy Spirit into a man's life can accomplish this miracle. The fact that God *slowed* Jacob's *pace* has everything to do with the *peace* this haunted man began to experience.

For further reflection:
1. Am I willing to "slow down" as Jacob did?
2. Does my nature need to be changed?
3. Have I ever had an experience with God such as Jacob had?

Slow me down, Lord, and help me to:

Be still, and know that I am God....

—Psalm 46:10

The world around us is chaotic and confused, threatening at any moment to break apart as a result of natural causes or because of man's mismanagement of his resources. The people who can cope with our modern madness are those who can remain calm in the eye of the storm. And their secret strength lies in their knowledge of God. Old Aaron Arrowsmith (1750–1823) told a story that pinpoints this truth for the believer: "A heathen philosopher once asked a Christian, 'Where is God?' The Christian answered, 'Let me first ask you, Where is He not?'" As Christians we can know that God is everywhere present, and he has given us two avenues of approach to him—prayer and meditation in the Word. Bolstered by these two resources, I can move ahead in the calm assurance of knowing God.

For further thought:
1. Does the world "rattle" me with its clamor?
2. Do I have regular recourse to prayer and the Word that equips me to "survive" the pressures surrounding me?

In pursuit of God's peace, today I will:

Create in me a clean heart, O God; and renew a right spirit within me. Cast me not away from thy presence; and take not thy Holy Spirit from me. Restore unto me the joy of thy salvation; and uphold me with thy free spirit.

—Psalm 51:10–12

Would I dare to pray as David does here? As I read these words I'm convicted of my own lack of dedication in my Christian walk. It's so easy to detour from the proper path the Lord would have me travel onto Satan's broad way. It can happen so subtly that I'm not even aware I'm on a detour—until suddenly I realize the "dirt" and shabby living I'm involved in. The "clean sense of God" I once knew has disappeared, and in its place I know dissatisfaction and unhappiness. My mask slips; I see behind it to the sadness within me and know that God needs to "renew a right spirit." That's when I'm reminded of Paul's words, "Now I rejoice, not that you were made sorry, but that ye sorrowed to repentance. . . ." (2 Cor. 7:9, 10). God wants to see that kind of sorrow in my life. Nothing can take the place of his Spirit within me. It's the only place to experience "the joy of thy salvation." Lord, open my heart and my eyes to my true condition—and perform your divine surgery in my life. "Create in me a clean heart, O God!"

For further reflection:
1. Am I on a detour now—or am I in God's will for my life?
2. What would God have me to do next?

As I open myself to you, Lord, work in my life to:

But the angel said to him, "Do not be afraid, Zechariah, for your prayer is heard, and your wife Elizabeth will bear you a son, and you shall call his name John. And you will have joy and gladness, and many will rejoice at his birth; for he will be great before the Lord . . . *and he will be filled with the Holy Spirit. . . ."*

　　　　　　　　　　　—Luke 1:12–15, RSV, emphasis mine

"Great before the Lord." At first glance this would appear to be a commendation of John—but there's a deeper meaning in these words. John was great because he was in "the sight of the Lord" (KJV). Only those are great whom God has made so. The secret of their power is that they stand in the sight of the Lord. There is a borrowed glow upon them. If they get out of his presence, like the mighty Samson they lose their strength and become as other men. The secret of John's strength lay in the fact that he was "filled with the Holy Spirit." Not even Moses was greater than John in that respect. John stands in the first rank of the spiritually great, not because of who he is, but because of who God is, within him. There's a lesson for me here!

For further reflection:
1. Do I live as though I were "in the sight of the Lord" every moment of the day and night?
2. Do I know any Christian who seems to "stand tall" in the sight of the Lord?

Lord, I want to stand tall in your sight today, which means I must:

He made my mouth like a sharp sword, in the shadow of his hand he hid me; he made me a polished arrow, in his quiver he hid me away. And he said to me, "You are my servant, Israel, in whom I will be glorified."

—Isaiah 49:2, 3, RSV

This passage speaks of the coming Messiah, Jesus Christ born in Bethlehem, but the truth expressed is applicable to *every* Christian. The heavenly Father has given us every work and privilege conferred upon the Savior except for the activities of the Atonement. Proof of that is found in Jesus' statement, "As thou has sent me into the world, even so have I also sent them into the world" (John 17:18). In Isaiah's day, each soldier had his own favorite weapon, his "polished arrow." Think of it: "He made *me* a polished arrow." How awesome to know that God can make me a "polished arrow" to his glory. This speaks of being finely tuned, superbly balanced, of the very best quality. Such workmanship requires time and supreme skill. Such a perfect weapon always functions at its finest because it is designed and built to do so. Every crisis situation brings out the best in God's favorite tools—his children. This is the way I can and will glorify him—by being a servant.

For further reflection:
1. Fine tools are polished by being put to use. Am I being polished?
2. What specific "polishing" do I need?

Lord, I want to be a polished servant in your hand. Today I will:

Whosoever shall do the will of God, the same is my brother, and my sister, and mother.

—Mark 3:35

Jesus is expressing a concept here too vast for me to grasp. Elsewhere in this book we've talked about relationships and how deeply involved we humans are in them. But think of the implications here: imagine being as closely related to Jesus as a brother or sister. Then Jesus gives expression to an even deeper relationship—that of mother and child. Somehow it's difficult for me to picture myself that closely related to the Son of God, Jesus Christ. But way back in the Old Testament Solomon said, "There are friends who pretend to be friends, but there is a friend who sticks closer than a brother" (Proverbs 18:24, RSV). I like to capitalize that word *friend* and think of it as a reference to Jesus in my life. What is the key to this close relationship? Obedience, for the first part of today's verse reports, "whosoever shall *do* the will of God." As I obey, and then make it a daily, ongoing practice to continue obeying, I am drawn into a closer and closer relationship with my Elder Brother.

For further reflection:
1. As I think of my close "family" relationship to Jesus, does it make any difference in the way I live?
2. Is there an area of disobedience coming between me and my Savior?

Lord, I'm overwhelmed at the thought of my relationship to you. It makes me want to:

My sheep hear my voice, and I know them, and they follow me; and I give them eternal life, and they shall never perish, and no one shall snatch them out of my hand.

—John 10:27, 28, RSV

In these few words, Jesus was spelling out a way for his followers to gauge their spiritual growth. In a word this passage gives one criterion—the ability to "hear" the Lord's voice. Actually the ability to hear God's voice is the key to spiritual discernment. I don't believe Christians have ever lived in a time when spiritual discernment was more vital. Another gauge for growth in grace is listed in the next phrase: "they follow me." Discernment implies a further step—obedience to the truth perceived. As I hitch obedience to discernment I intensify my ability to hear. My spiritual ears become sharper as I obey—or I become dull of hearing as I disobey. Disobedience blocks my spiritual ears to the point that God has to shout at me to get my attention. Two parallel promises are then given to the listening Christian: "I give unto them eternal life" and "they shall never perish." Jesus then adds, "No one shall snatch them out of my hand." Lord, give me a listening and obedient ear!

For further reflection:
1. Am I in a position to "hear" my Shepherd's voice?
2. Do I "follow" him as I should—or do I choose my own path?

Lord, let my life be lived in obedience to you. Today I will:

For the moment all discipline seems painful rather than pleasant; later it yields the peaceful fruit of righteousness to those who have been trained by it.

—Hebrews 12:11, RSV

All of us encounter chastening at one point or another in our Christian lives. Sometimes it's a matter of our having to give up our "good things" to make room for God's best. I am convinced that God has a plan for my life. What I need to do is look to him and listen to his message to me, letting his discipline in my life chip away at me until his plan emerges clearly. It's as if my life were a shapeless chunk of marble. It can remain that way—useless and not too interesting to look at. Or I can allow God to creatively chisel the useless part away until he makes something beautiful out of what is left. If you've ever watched a sculptor at work, you noticed that in the early stages of his efforts he may work quickly and remove large chunks—but the closer he comes to completing his task, the more careful and cautious he is. In the final stages, he sometimes removes only tiny pieces after careful consideration. In a sense, I think God might sometimes work like that, too. I wonder how big the chunks he next removes will be. Will I then yield "the peaceful fruit of righteousness"?

For further reflection:
1. When was the last time I became aware of God's chastening hand?
2. Is it lighter or heavier now?

Lord, shape my life according to your plan. Today I will:

18 NOVEMBER

Without faith it is impossible to please him. For whoever would draw near to God must believe that he exists and that he rewards those who seek him. By faith Noah, being warned by God concerning events as yet unseen, took heed and constructed an ark for the saving of his household; by this he condemned the world and became an heir of the righteousness which comes by faith.

—Hebrews 11:6, 7, RSV

Noah's faith never ceases to amaze and shame me. He stood alone in surroundings that must have been as bad or worse than mine—and he dared to put God first in a world that denied God's existence. Do I have that kind of daring commitment? Immortal Martin Luther did a lot of counseling with those who joined the early Protestant reform movement. When people with problems came to him, he would counsel: "Let God be God." That's what Noah courageously did—and I need to do it too. If I am giving God his proper place in my life, it won't be "I and God"; it will be "God and I." I cannot expect God to lead me if he's not out in front in my life as he was in Noah's. And whoever heard of a guide leading from behind?

For further thought:
1. What place do I give God in my life?
2. How would I have handled the command God gave to Noah?

Lord, I want you to be the leader in my life. Today I will:

My little children, I am writing this to you so that you may not sin; but if anyone does sin, we have an advocate with the Father, Jesus Christ the righteous.

—1 John 2:1, RSV

Dwight L. Moody once said, "There are two ways of covering sin—man's way and God's way." The difference, he pointed out, is that sin covered in man's way is not buried at all—but sin covered by God is buried for good, never to be uncovered again. As a finite man I cannot grasp the magnitude of that redemption. *How* God can forgive me I do not need to understand. All I need to do is accept the fact of that forgiveness. Then I should live a life worthy of his calling, knowing I have an "advocate with the father, Jesus Christ the righteous."

For further reflection:
1. What do I usually try to do with my "sins"?
2. What would God have me do with my sins (see 1 John 1:9)?

Lord, today I confess that:

No one can serve two masters; for either he will hate the one and love the other, or he will be devoted to the one and despise the other.
—Matthew 6:24, RSV

Both Jesus and Paul are articulating a vital and vast spiritual truth in these passages: It's impossible to walk both sides of the street at once—and there's no way to walk the center line successfully. You'll get run over in traffic for sure. As Joshua discovered, the pilgrim must "choose" (24:15) whom he will serve. Divided service is not an option, for the devil soon envelops the part-time servant. Judas Iscariot learned this lesson to his doom. Mary chose "that good part" (Luke 10:42) in sitting at the feet of Jesus. The apostle Paul, too, could say, "This one thing I do" and "For me to live is Christ." He concentrated on and chose to follow Jesus rather than man, refusing to make room in his life for Satan to get a foothold. This "singleness of mind" is the only way to peace and prosperity in the Christian life. Singleness of purpose is the path to spiritual success.

For further thought:
1. If I follow this "single" path, will I be guilty of having a "one-track mind"?
2. What is distracting me right now from single-minded service?

Lord, today I yield _____ to you. Help me to:

And he said to them, "Come away by yourselves to a lonely place, and rest a while." For many were coming and going, and they had no leisure even to eat.

—Mark 6:31, RSV

In some ways this passage breaks my heart, for it exposes, for all to see, an ailment that afflicts too many of us Christians. Somehow we can't seem to find time for sufficient fellowship with God and meditation on the Word; we shove communion with our heavenly Father to a back burner. As a result, hearts are hardened (see v. 52) for lack of spiritual rest. A man who rarely takes time to breathe deeply—or who lives in an atmosphere where it is unsafe to breathe deeply—is not a truly healthy man. And the same is true in the spiritual realm. Just as the physical man must learn habitually to breathe deeply, so the one who seeks spiritual health must take time to make deep spiritual breathing a habit. While I cannot always "come away" to a lonely place physically, I can foster in my life a spiritual atmosphere that will favor fellowship with my Father.

For further reflection:
1. Am I giving spiritual concerns proper priority in my life?
2. Do I have a "place" where I can commune with my Father?

Today I will:

Pilate said to them, "You have a guard of soldiers; go, make it as secure as you can."

—Matthew 27:65, RSV

There's a powerful truth left unspoken in this passage. What foresight into future events caused Pilate to qualify his command to the chief priest and Pharisees by the phrase, "as secure as you can"? Ordinarily, with any normal man, it would not be necessary to "guard" a corpse to keep it in the grave. Did Pilate possibly have a haunting suspicion that Jesus might be able to rise from the dead? Actually, Jesus could not be boxed up inside a sealed tomb any more than his Spirit can be captured within a label or a denomination today. The sealing of the tomb was simply the inauguration of his post-resurrection ministry, for he rose again in spite of all men could do to retain him in the grave. As a Christian, I marvel at and rejoice in the awesome power resident in my Savior and Lord. How victorious my life could be if I turned that power loose in me, if I dared to surrender completely to him.

For further reflection:
1. Do I really believe Jesus has the power to rise from the dead?
2. Am I experiencing that power in my life?
3. What is getting in the way of this power for me?

Lord, today open my eyes to your power that I might:

He is not here; for he has risen, as he said. Come, see the place where he lay.

—Matthew 28:6, RSV

I find this entire chapter tremendously exciting and fast moving—and it suggests a life motto which I'm not sure is original with me: "Let me live each day as though Jesus had died yesterday, had risen this morning, and was coming back again tomorrow." That's cramming a lot into a few short words, but in a sense that's the way God looks at my life. His time frame telescopes a thousand years into a day; he sees the end from the beginning. He knows all about me and loves me anyway. If I really realized this, would it make a difference in the way I live? If I really lived my life in this constant awareness of his presence, his all-seeing eye on my every move, what would I do differently?

For further reflection:
1. What is my life motto at this moment?
2. To what do I devote my life's energy and resources?
3. What changes do I need to make to live according to this new motto?

Lord, let me live my life in this all-encompassing awareness of your presence. Today I will:

24 NOVEMBER

The Lord knows the way of the righteous, but the way of the wicked will perish.

—Psalm 1:6, RSV

I spent most of my adult life in the North, so I know what it means to see roads "break up" as the aftermath of a harsh, cold winter. But then I moved to warmer climes—and I discovered that roads "break up" here in Texas as well. Really, it's simply the difference between a "good" and "bad" roadbed. A "bad" road has a poor, an inferior foundation—the roadbed is really prepared of "wood, hay and stubble." A "good" road, on the other hand, has a solid foundation, a well-prepared "way." Jesus said, "I am the way." That is the good road. Its Builder and Maker is God. Outward circumstances do not affect its condition, for it is perfectly prepared.

For further thought:
1. What "way" am I walking?
2. On what kind of a foundation am I building my life?

Lord, help me today to:

The horse is made ready for the day of battle, but the victory belongs to the Lord.

—Proverbs 21:31, RSV

A gospel song title—"Victory in Jesus"—leaps into my mind when I read this proverb. And another verse of scripture, too: "This is the victory that overcometh the world, even our faith" (1 John 5:4). I love horses, and think they are among the noblest creatures God ever created; this verse first caught my eye for that reason. But then I began to grasp the rich meaning of the rest of the verse: "... victory belongs to the Lord." The person who really believes this will not be bothered by anxiety. Someone has said, "An optimist sees an opportunity in every calamity, a pessimist a calamity in every opportunity." An optimist is exhilarated by the thought of battle when the Lord is in it—a pessimist is scared and defeated before the battle even begins.

For further reflection:
1. What kind of Christian am I—optimist or pessimist?
2. Do I really believe *all* of this verse?

Lord, help me today to:

It was at this time that disciples came to Jesus with the question, "Who is really greatest in the kingdom of Heaven?"
—Matthew 18:1, PHILLIPS

What does it mean to be a disciple? Jesus spells it out pretty plainly here, but I'm still finding out what it means on a day-by-day, nitty-gritty basis. Can I be a born-again believer without becoming a wholehearted follower? Can an individual be lukewarm as a church can (Rev. 3:16)? In Matthew 10:42, Jesus said, "Believe me, anyone who gives even a drink of water to one of these little ones, just because he is my disciple, will by no means lose his reward" (PHILLIPS). That brings it down to where I live. Just talking about being a Christian doesn't make me one. Practical Christianity has to do with ministering to widows and orphans, says James (1:27). And Jesus said, "By their fruits ye shall know them." Just as we can know a tree on the basis of the kind of fruit it bears, we can know a Christian by the kind of deeds he does.

For further reflection:

1. As others look at my life, what kind of disciple do they see?
2. What can I *do* today to show whose disciple I am?

As your disciple today, Lord, I will:

*I don't even value my opinion of myself. For I might be quite igno-
rant of any fault in myself—but that doesn't justify me before God.
My only true judge is the Lord.*

—1 Corinthians 4:4, PHILLIPS

Paul's love for the Corinthians emerges strongly in this passage—
and his humanness does as well. His sarcasm becomes pretty apparent from verse 8 on. Josh Billings, the American humorist (his real
name was Henry Wheeler Shaw and he lived from 1818 to 1885),
once said: "It's better to know nothing than to know what ain't so."
That bit of homely philosophy parallels Paul's words to the Corinthians. He claimed no superior knowledge for himself—but wanted them to do the same. In a sense, Paul is calling for all of us to
keep an open mind in the spiritual realm, for as soon as we claim to
"know it all" spiritually, then we've ceased to grow and develop.

For further consideration:
1. Am I ever a spiritual "know-it-all"?
2. Am I ever tempted to "lord it over" others?
3. If so, what can I do about it?

**Lord, help me to be open and vulnerable to your leading in
my life. Today I will:**

If we have food and clothing, with these we shall be content.
—1 Timothy 6:8, RSV

In another epistle, Paul gave expression to this same sentiment: "I have learned, in whatsoever state I am, therewith to be content" (Phil. 4:11). The writer to the Hebrews also said: "Be content with such things as ye have" (13:5). Sir James Scott added his word of wisdom: "No man is so sad as he who has much and wants more." What a description of most of us today! The more we have, the more we strive to gain additional material things. As Christians, we should be satisfied with our *needs* being met, but instead too often we expect our *desires* to be fulfilled as well.

For further reflection:
1. Am I living in "godliness with contentment"?
2. What *needs* do I have that God is not meeting?
3. What *desires* do I have that I expect God to supply?

Lord, you have been so good to me. In light of that I will:

NOVEMBER 29

To him that overcometh will I give to eat of the tree of life....
—Revelation 2:7

Oh, that I might stand for Christ in the crisis! Jim Elliott, martyred missionary to the Auca Indians, prayed at the age of 20: "Father, make of me a crisis man. Bring those I contact to decision. Let me not be a milepost on a single road; make me a fork that men must turn one way or another on facing Christ in me." This is the prayer of a daring and dedicated man. It reflects a spirit too often lacking among modern-day Christians, although it must have been rather widespread among the early followers of Jesus. At least, some of them turned their world upside down (Acts 17:6). Lord, make me to stand tall in the crisis. The failure is not with God, it is with me!

For further reflection:
1. Would I dare to pray a prayer like this?
2. In the light of the kind of life I'm living, could I authentically pray such a prayer?

Lord, I'm speechless before you, but help me to:

30 NOVEMBER

Read Exodus 24:12–18

Then Moses went up on the mountain, and the cloud covered the mountain. The glory of the Lord settled on Mount Sinai, and the cloud covered it six days; and on the seventh day he called to Moses out of the midst of the cloud.

—Exodus 24:15, 16, RSV

It must have been difficult for Moses, who was leading a vast multitude of people, to spend seven days in the dark in this manner. A seventeenth-century mystic, Don Miguel de Molinas (1640–1697), saw the whole experience in this light: "When God had a mind to instruct his own captain, Moses, and give him two tables written in stone, he called him up to a mountain. At that time, *God being there with him,* the mountain was darkened and environed with thick clouds. Moses was standing idle, in the gloom, not knowing what to think or say. Seven days after, God commanded Moses to come to the top of the mountain wherein he showed him his glory, and filled him with great consolation!" Seven days in the dark. This reveals to me a vital spiritual truth. From Moses I learn that every dark passage is but a corridor through which faith passes on its way to sight. There's a light at the end of the tunnel. But even more importantly, my Savior and Guide is with me *in* the tunnel!

For further thought:
1. What other experience of Bible characters bears out this truth of God's presence (i.e., Daniel, Job, Joseph, etc.)?
2. When was the last time I was "on the mountain" with God?

Lord, today I will:

DECEMBER 1

Therefore confess your sins to one another, and pray for one another that you may be healed. The prayer of a righteous man has great power in its effects.

—James 5:16, RSV

In Proverbs 15:18, 19, the writer says, "A wrathful man stirreth up strife; but he that is slow to anger appeaseth strife. The way of the slothful man is a hedge of thorns: but the way of the righteous is made plain." It is obvious that God is interested in the lifestyles and attitudes of those who call on him in prayer. E. M. Bounds (1835–1913), who is noted for his devotional writings and particularly his books on prayer, said: "What the church needs today is not more machinery or better, not new organizations or more and novel methods, but men whom the Holy Ghost can use—men of prayer, men mighty in prayer. The Holy Ghost does not flow through methods, but through men. He does not come on machinery but on men. He does not anoint plans, but men—men of prayer." A truly righteous man is not *self*-righteous; he is bathed in the righteousness of Christ through the filling of the Holy Spirit. Are my prayers having "great power in their effects"?

For further thought:
1. Is prayer a natural part of my life?
2. Do I pray specifically?
3. Have I had my prayers answered?

Lord, today I want to pray specifically for:

2 DECEMBER

Glancing this way and that and seeing no one, he killed the Egyptian and hid him in the sand.

—Exodus 2:12, NIV

Moses teaches us a profound spiritual lesson here. Although he had been brought up in a godly Israelite home, he had also been exposed to the seamy side of life in Pharaoh's palace (v. 10). When he saw one of his Israelite brothers being beaten, he looked in every direction but the right one—up! Angry at the Egyptian for mistreating the Israelite, he killed him without looking to the One from whom he should have taken his orders. Am I sometimes like that? Do I fail to look up to my Commander-in-Chief for orders? Am I prone to take matters into my own hands—jumping to conclusions and "flying off the handle" rather than "fleeing to my Savior"? I think Moses made a mistake here and got ahead of God's will for him because of his impetuous action. And it's a danger for me as well—I, too, can get ahead of God if I'm not careful to look up to him for daily direction.

For further thought:
1. Have I ever moved ahead in haste like Moses did—and then repented at leisure?
2. Was Moses wrong in killing the Egyptian?
3. What might Moses have done instead of slaying the Egyptian?

I've been like Moses here in that I have:

DECEMBER 3

And if thy hand offend thee, cut if off: it is better for thee to enter into life maimed, than having two hands to go into hell, into the fire that never shall be quenched.

—Mark 9:43

In the evaluation of eternity, which is most important—physical health or spiritual wholeness? On God's scale of values, physical disability is to be desired rather than spiritual incompleteness. There is great concern abroad today for physical fitness. It sometimes seems that everywhere I look I see joggers. No neighborhood is complete without its cadre of dedicated runners—from early morning until late at night. There's nothing wrong with this, but I wonder if we're equally concerned for our spiritual well-being? I don't think Jesus meant us to take this admonition recorded here in Mark literally, but as old Matthew Henry said, "It is better to lose the eye and the hand ... than to give way to a sin and perish eternally in it."

For further thought:
1. Is there something in my life I should "cut off"?
2. With which part of me am I most tempted to sin—my hands, eyes, or feet?

Lord, today I will cut out of my life:

4 DECEMBER

Read Ecclesiastes 5:1–7

Guard your steps when you go to the house of God; to draw near to listen is better than to offer the sacrifice of fools. . . . Be not rash with your mouth nor let your heart be hasty to utter a word before God . . . therefore let your words be few.

—Ecclesiastes 5:1, 2, RSV

Some people, myself included, talk too much. I need to remember to "think first, say later." I'll never be forced to explain away embarrassing words if I don't say them. Silence does not give away my ignorance, but talking might. These are lessons I need to learn. I cannot put my foot in my closed mouth—but it's all too easy to do it if my mouth instead of my ears is open. I wonder how many messages from the Lord I've missed because my mouth instead of my mind was busy. And how many times have my "empty words" hurt rather than helped those who hear them?

For further thought:
1. Do I listen more than I speak?
2. Is it possible to be too quiet?
3. How am I going to use my words today?

Lord, today I'll exercise a listening ear and I will:

DECEMBER 5

The Lord went before them by day in a pillar of cloud to lead them along the way, and by night in a pillar of fire to give them light, that they might travel by day and by night.

—Exodus 13:21, RSV

The world today is crying out for authoritative leadership. Everywhere we look there is a vacuum of authentic authority in the ranks of human leadership. So where do we look for guidance? The soul's eternal cry is for the God who can give it direction and leadership. We do not know the way we take. Life has too many options to permit us complete confidence in our choice of a path. A visible token of God's presence would hearten and encourage us. We should then have no doubt as to our course. But may not the ancient pillar of flame and cloud be, after all, a symbol or just-as-real divine leadership? To those who have eyes to see his sign, God's presence is just as clear as of old.

For further reflection:
1. How do I see God leading me today?
2. Am I truly willing to follow his leadership?

Under your leadership today, Lord, I will:

6 DECEMBER

Hear my voice in accordance with your love; renew my life, O Lord, according to your laws.

—Psalm 119:149, NIV

This verse tells me that I do God an injustice when I fail to come to him in prayer. John Ruskin says, "We treat God with irreverence by banishing him from our thoughts, not by referring to his will on slight occasions.... There is nothing so small but that we may honor God by asking his guidance of it, or insult him by taking it into our own hands." So often I think I should not "bother God" with my little concerns, but the Psalmist didn't let that deter him. He was in constant communication with his God, and shared his inner complaints as well as his outward praise. I need to be just as open with God—just as willing to express my frustration as my faith. Then, and only then, will my Christianity be the "faith for the marketplace."

For further reflection:
1. Am I ever too busy to "bother" God with my concerns?
2. Do I pray as if God can read my mind (and he can)—or do I sometimes "cover up" my real feelings?

Lord, today I'm really concerned about:

DECEMBER 7

Put on then, as God's chosen ones, holy and beloved, compassion, kindness, lowliness, meekness, and patience, forbearing one another and, if one has a complaint against another, forgiving each other; as the Lord has forgiven you, so you also must forgive.

—Colossians 3:12, 13, RSV

This is a passage that deserves to be read alongside the apostle Paul's classic listing of Christian virtues in Galatians 5:22, 23. It contains the secret of soul serenity which Jesus knew and shared with his disciples: practice loving your neighbor instead of hating him. Paul here also echoes his advice to the Ephesians: "Let all bitterness, and wrath, and anger, and clamour, and evil speaking, be put away from you, with all malice" (4:31). It would be well for me to take up this passage at the beginning of the day to get my heart ready for the struggles and even the enmity which could potentially arise in my relationships with family, friends, and business acquaintances. Anger is a very real part of our modern pressurized lifestyle. If I can recognize its appearance before the fact, prepare for it in advance, and put it to rest at that point, I'll be better able to handle whatever comes—coolly and with Christian calmness. I need to remember that anger against a fellow struggler is also enmity against God. That's why I must consciously call upon him to "abide with me" so that I can "abide in him."

For further thought:

1. Am I consciously "putting on God" when I rise to meet the day?
2. What does it mean to keep "short accounts" with God—and do I do it?

Today I will:

8 DECEMBER

He only is my rock and my salvation: he is my defense; I shall not be moved. In God is my salvation and my glory; the rock of my strength and my refuge is in God.

—Psalm 62:6, 7

Throughout the Scriptures there are symbols or types of God which illustrate his attributes, but none is more striking than this one so often used by the psalmist David: "God is my rock." What a picture of strength, solidarity, and stability this is. Anyone who has seen the "mighty rocks" of the Holy Land will know what David had in mind here. A rock in the desert can serve as a shelter from a scorching sun or other enemy from above, as a bulwark against the rushing wind below, as a platform that withstands the sudden flood. All these God is to his children, but he is also a defense, a "fortress" against the foe. His Word is both a weapon of defense and offense. And this mighty One is *my* God!

For further thought:
1. Am I really living as though God were my "rock"?
2. What is happening in my life right now that is leading me to "lean" on the Rock?

Since I know God is my rock, today I will:

Be not slothful, but followers of them who through faith and patience inherit the promises.

—Hebrews 6:12

Let us learn from this communion of saints to live in hope. Those who are now at rest were once like ourselves. They were once weak, faulty, sinful; they had their burdens and hindrances, their slumbering and weariness, their failures and their falls. But now they have overcome. Their life was once homely and commonplace. Their day ran out as ours. Morning and noon and night came and went to them as to us. Little fretful circumstances and frequent disturbing changes wasted away their hours as ours. There is nothing in our life that was not in theirs; there was nothing in theirs but may be also in our own. They have overcome, each one, and one by one; each in his turn, when the day came, and God called him to the trial. And so shall we likewise.

H. E. MANNING (1808–1892)

For further thought:
1. Do I sometimes forget the "big picture" as I fight today's little battle?
2. As I look at those Christians who have gone on before, who stands out as one who truly inherited the promises?

Lord, today I remember _____ and how he/she overcame. His/her secret was:

10 DECEMBER

Jesus felt genuine love for this man as he looked at him. "You lack only one thing," he told him; "go and sell all you have and give the money to the poor and you shall have treasure in heaven and come, follow me." Then the man's face fell, and he went sadly away, for he was very rich.

—Mark 10:21, 22, LB

During his earthly pilgrimage, Jesus met and mingled with many people. Among them was this well-meaning man whose wealth got in his way. He turned "sadly away," and he missed a great opportunity. He came reverently to Christ in a proper attitude of humility, his spirit teachable and eager to hear wisdom from Jesus' lips. But when Jesus gave him the key to spiritual wealth, the rich young ruler let his material wealth deflect him from eternal riches. I wonder if we, too, don't grieve our Master more by our refusal to follow his best for us than by our positive violations of God's law. This shows another side of sin—the deeds of omission rather than commission. Our hesitancy to answer the supreme opportunity with a supreme consecration is no less fatal to our soul than is gross sin. Only in the final audit of character shall we know what losses we have sustained through disobedience to our heavenly visions.

For further reflection:
1. Have I, like the laudable young man in this passage, been "disobedient to the heavenly vision" (see Acts 26:19)?
2. Why was the apostle Paul's response to Christ's call different?

Lord, today you have told me to:

DECEMBER 11

For this is the message that ye heard from the beginning, that we should love one another.

—1 John 3:11

We may, if we choose, make the worst of one another. Every one has his weak points; every one has his faults; we may make the worst of these; we may fix our attention constantly upon these. But we may also make the best of one another. We may forgive, even as we hope to be forgiven. We may put ourselves in the place of others, and ask what we should wish to be done to us, and thought of us, were we in their place. By loving whatever is lovable in those around us, love will flow back from them to us, and life will become a pleasure instead of a pain; and earth will become like heaven; and we shall become not unworthy followers of him whose name is Love.

A. P. STANLEY (1815–1882)

For further thought:
1. Is there someone in my life right now who especially needs my love?
2. Is there someone I'm hurting by my lack of love?

Lord, today I will love:

He knoweth the way that I take.... Thou knowest my downsitting and mine uprising, thou understandeth my thought afar off. Thou compassest my path and my lying down, and art acquainted with all my ways.

—Job 23:10; Psalm 129:2, 3

We complain of the slow, dull life we are forced to lead, of our humble sphere of action, of our low position in the scale of society, of having no room to make ourselves known, of our wasted energies, of our years of patience. So do we say that we have no Father who is directing our life; so do we say that God has forgotten us; so do we boldly judge what life is best for us; and so by our complaining do we lose the use and profit of the quiet years. O men of little faith! Because you are not sent out yet into your labor, do you think God has ceased to remember you? Because you are forced to be outwardly inactive, do you think you, also, may not be, in your years of quiet, "about your Father's business"? It is a period given to us in which to mature ourselves for the work which God will give us to do.

STOPFORD A. BROOKE (1832–1916)

For further thought:
1. Am I guilty of "little faith"?
2. Have I had, or am I now having, a period of relative quiet in which to do some "growing"?

In view of God's presence with me, today I will:

*The Lord appeared to us in the past, saying: "I have loved you with
an everlasting love; I have drawn you with loving kindness."*
—Jeremiah 31:3, NIV

This verse in Jeremiah and the other passages cited unveil the
secret of God's life, which is love. My life, insofar as it is spiritual, is
simply my response to that love in the active prompting of my soul
of which God himself is both author and source. The initiative is
always with him—not with me. Before my faith, my prayer, the
forgiveness of my sin, my act of kindness, my love toward another—there must be God! Before I begin my search for him, he is
already out watching for me, as we see the father pictured in the
parable of the prodigal son in Matthew 21. I may think I have
discovered an exciting new truth, but he has been there before me.
He is the One who reveals it—not I. This is what it means to know
that "underneath are the everlasting arms" (Deut. 33:27)! In everlasting love God is joining me to himself.

For further thought:
1. Am I living daily in the awareness of these tremendous
   truths?
2. Does my life reflect this love to others—those close to me
   and those with whom I have only casual contact?

Lord, in the light of your everlasting love I will:

14 DECEMBER

Many waters cannot quench love, neither can the floods drown it. . . .
—Song of Solomon 8:7

Many meanings are lumped together in the modern term, "love." But biblically the highest form or kind of love is agape love—giving love. This kind of selfless love is best personified by Christ on the cross—his sacrifice of himself is the ultimate gift of love. Some anonymous wise man has said, "Love is the doorway through which the human soul passes from selfishness to service." Love is also the great revealer. We cannot truly know another person until we have learned to love—and we cannot truly know love until we have met the Giver and Sustainer of love—God. That is why both Solomon in the Old Testament and Paul in the New see love as central to the godly walk. This is why, I believe, the Christian couple has the best chance to survive the pressures placed upon the marriage relationship. A great teacher, working to understand and explain life by reason, found that the heart had reasons which the reason did not know. It is in our loves and our loyalties that God makes his most intimate and revealing contacts with our souls.

For further thought:
1. What kind of love dominates my relationship with my spouse or with my family?
2. Do I love as God loved me, unconditionally—or is my love conditioned by what others do or say to me?

If I am to have the kind of love Solomon describes, I must find it by:

O Lord, hear me praying; listen to my plea, O God my King, for I will never pray to anyone but you.

—Psalm 5:1, 2, LB

David's prayer here is humble and heartfelt. How he pleads with God to hear and answer the deep stirrings of his heart. Maltbie Babcock (1858–1901) was talking about this kind of earnest prayer when he wrote: "Prayer must mean something to us if it is to mean anything to God. If the accustomed time of prayer comes around and we have nothing that interests us enough to pray about definitely and honestly, we would better frankly say so to God than kill time in hollow, heartless formality. To keep up the habit of prayer by saying thoughtless words is not worthwhile. It is a bad habit of prayer, or it is a habit of bad prayer. It is better not to pray than to pray and not be honest. This prayer, however, at least might be always possible: 'O God! show me my need of Thee.'"

For further thought:
1. How do my prayers stack up with those of David?
2. When is the last time I really pled with God in prayer?

Lord, today I specifically pray for:

Lord, teach us to pray.

—Luke 11:1

The law of cause and effect operates in the spiritual realm as well as in the natural world. Faith and prayer afford a good illustration of this. We cannot pray without faith, yet we cannot have faith without prayer. Each is cause for the other. But we need not hesitate to accept both faith and prayer on this basis, for it is proved out in our daily life. We learn to trust a friend by simply trusting him. Our faith in him grows as our friendship deepens, and our friendship deepens with our growing faith. Thus faith in God comes by companionship with him in the practice of his presence in prayer, and his companionship grows more real and sure and comforting as our faith takes deeper root in our souls.

For further thought:

1. Are my prayers lifted up by faith—or do they stop at the ceiling?
2. What can I do to strengthen my prayer life and build up my faith?

My specific prayer of faith for today is:

I do not seek my own glory.

—John 8:50, RSV

Ours is a day which worships aggression. We almost admire the hard-driving executive type who rolls over the feelings and the opinions of "smaller" people. The powerful personality is worshiped. Jesus' words of meekness and humility, "I do not seek my own glory," would be ridiculed in today's society, just as they were in the first century. Yet as we study our Lord's character we see how closely related are true humility and real power. Great as he was, far-reaching and vast as his purpose appeared, he nevertheless remained cognizant of his brotherly relationship to all men and his personal subjection to the will of God. He thus knew that greatness and power would be obtained not by proudly seeking to be ministered to, but by unselfishly giving his life in helpful service.

For further thought:
1. Can I honestly speak the words Jesus spoke, "I do not seek my own glory"?
2. In what ways do I look for personal recognition?

In the light of Jesus' humility, today I will:

All the paths of the Lord are mercy and truth unto such as keep his covenant and his testimonies.

—Psalm 25:10

It is not by seeking more fertile regions where toil is lighter— happier circumstances free from difficult complications and troublesome people—but by bringing the high courage of a devout soul, clear in principle and aim, to bear upon what is given to us, that we brighten our inward light, lead something of a true life, and introduce the kingdom of heaven into the midst of our earthly day. If we cannot work out the will of God where God has placed us, then why has He placed us there?

J. H. THOM (1808–1894)

For further thought:
1. Am I working out the will of God where he has placed me?
2. Is there anything about my circumstances that can hinder my truly serving God?

To work out your will in my life, Lord, today I will:

DECEMBER 19

I had fainted, unless I had believed to see the goodness of the Lord in the land of the living.

—Psalm 27:13

Let us be very careful of thinking, on the one hand, that we have no work assigned us to do, or, on the other hand, that what we have assigned to us is not the right thing for us. If ever we can say in our hearts to God, in reference to any daily duty, "This is not my place; I would choose something dearer; I am capable of something higher"; we are guilty not only of rebellion, but of blasphemy. It is equivalent to saying, not only, "My heart revolts against Thy commands," but "Thy commands are unwise; Thine Almighty guidance is unskilful; Thine omniscient eye has mistaken the capacities of Thy creature; Thine infinite love is indifferent to the welfare of Thy child."

ELIZABETH CHARLES (1827–1896)

For further thought:
1. Have I ever dared to talk to God as David does here? Or as Mrs. Charles does?
2. Have my actions ever spoken out the way Mrs. Charles describes?

Lord, today my honest prayer is:

20 DECEMBER

You also must be ready; for the Son of Man is coming in an unexpected hour.

—Luke 12:40, RSV

We need always to be watchful and prepared for whatever comes. True character is always built in the midst of peril. In this world, at least, I can't expect to reach a point of perfection where my soul is secure from the possibility of failure and defeat. Even those who have walked a lifetime as a Christian must be continually on their guard against the strategies of Satan. This involves not only *defense* against Satan's subtle temptations, but also *offense* as I prepare myself spiritually to meet the opportunities of service and growth. The truly Christian personality doesn't just happen automatically. It doesn't grow uncultivated. It is the *product* of what is going on in the life. Our Lord constantly knocks at our heart's door. Happy are we if we hear his knock and open to him!

For further thought:
1. What is happening in my life right now that can help me grow?
2. Has Christ knocked at my heart's door lately?

Lord, next time I hear you knocking I will:

Blessed is the man who endures trial, for when he has stood the test he will receive the crown of life which God has promised to those who love him.

         —James 1:12, RSV

I should not be among those who resent temptation. Rather, I should stand with my Lord, who willingly met the tempter and resisted him. If I resent temptation, I lose the possibility and potential of glory and strength of character that can come only through such testing. Paul said, "Count it all joy when ye fall into divers temptations." He meant that by resisting temptations we grow in grace and character—as we could not grow were our lives set in protected places where temptations could not come. My temptation is my *chance*—to win identity, character, and real comradeship with Christ. Lord, help me to look upon it in that light.

For further thought:
1. What temptations can I build upon?
2. Where do I go from here?

My temptation is in this direction:

22 DECEMBER

But it is you, my equal, my companion, my familiar friend. We used to hold sweet converse together; within God's house we walked in fellowship.

—Psalm 55:13, 14, RSV

Friends can be fickle, as David learned and shares in these two psalms. But yet how colorless our lives would be without intimate earthly friends! Even Jesus, when he walked our world, felt the need for friendship, and surrounded himself with an inner circle of close friends—Peter, James, and John. They, along with the wider circle of disciples represented by the entire disciple band, were our Lord's friends. This inner circle of Peter, James, and John shared their Master's most intimate secrets, but even they abandoned him in the end. All, that is, except John, that closest one who described himself as "the disciple whom Jesus loved" (John 20:2; 21:7, 20). John stood at the cross beside Mary, the mother of Jesus, and she became as his own mother on that dreadful day. Lord, I thank you for my close friends!

For further thought:
1. What kind of friend am I?
2. Who is my closest earthly friend?
3 Do I go to Jesus as to a friend?

As a true friend, today I will:

Remove far from me falsehood and lying; give me neither poverty nor riches; feed me with the food that is needful for me.

—Proverbs 30:8, RSV

These are the wise words of Agur. We don't know much about him, aside from these words of Proverbs 30—but what he says here proves out in practice. Many of us live our lives under the delusion that in possessions and the satisfaction of unlimited desire lies contentment. Agur, to the contrary, foreshadows the words of Jesus in the Lord's Prayer, "Give us this day our daily bread" (Matt. 6:11). It is a great discovery when we learn that contentment and inner peace lie in the direction of self-control and moderation—that the inner riches of the Spirit are more to be prized than are temporal possessions. Unlimited self-indulgence leaves the soul sapped of all energy, weary of life, and dissatisfied. Moderation and restraint, on the other hand, have their reward in the buoyant spirit and unwearied zest for life. Lord, let me pray Agur's prayer from my heart.

For further thought:
1. Do I live as Agur would advise me?
2. Do I ask things for myself—or do I seek a contented spirit, thankful for God's goodness?

In the light of this passage in Proverbs, today I will:

24 DECEMBER

Read James 1:16–25

Every good and perfect gift is from above, coming down from the Father of the heavenly lights, who does not change like shifting shadows.

—James 1:17, NIV

Looked at in context, this admonition from James can be taken to mean the existence of *two* gifts: the very act of giving, and the gift itself. James didn't believe in a passive, laid-back kind of piety. He was an activist. He believed that not only are all the gifts which come our way from God, but the privilege of giving in the name of Jesus is also his gift. I should approach life thankful for the *privilege* of giving and sharing in the work of God.

For further consideration:
1. Do I see myself as a channel of God's goodness?
2. Is there something in my life that blocks the love of God from flowing out through me?

Lord, today let my life reveal your love as I:

Now the birth of Jesus Christ took place in this way....
—Matthew 1:18, RSV

It is Christ's birthday. In among all our festivities should come sweet thoughts of the love of God. The gifts we may receive should make us think of the greatest gift of all—when God gave his Son. Let us all try to make our Christmas very full of memories of Christ. Let the blessed love of Christ make a glad Christmas in our hearts, helping us to be like Christ himself in love, unselfishness, and forgiveness.

What Christ is to us we ought, in our human measure, to be to others. Christmas means love. Christ came to our world to pour divine kindness on weary, needy, perishing human lives. The Christmas spirit in our hearts should send us out on the same errand. There is need everywhere for love's ministry. We should learn the true Christmas lesson of gentle, thoughtful kindness to those we love and to all we meet in life's busy ways.

J. R. MILLER

For further thought:
1. What does Christmas Day really mean to me?
2. Do I live in the glow of the Christmas light every day of the year—or is my faith only a "sometime" thing?

Lord, with Christmas in my heart today I will:

26 DECEMBER

Read Psalm 139:1–12
and Romans 8:27

For the Lord searcheth all hearts....

—1 Chronicles 28:9

It's hard for me to grasp that God is everywhere, because I'm so limited by my mortality. As a finite being, I can't expect to grasp the enormity and infinity of the One who made me. To attain a satisfactory concept of God is most difficult for even the wisest. Yet most of us deserve rebuke because we do not allow our thought of God to grow with our mental growth; we carry our childhood ideas of God to our mature life. We think of God too much as "up there," when he is just as truly "down here." We may be sure that we shall find him wherever we go. We cannot flee him with our sins, nor need we go far to find him when we need comfort and healing.

For further thought:
1. Do I ever try to "flee" from God?
2. Do I live as though God were everywhere?

In the light of your continual presence, dear God, today I will:

DECEMBER 27

Blessed are they that keep his testimonies, and that seek him with the whole heart.

—Psalm 119:2

If God requires anything of us, we have no right to draw back under the pretext that we are liable to commit some fault in obeying. It is better to obey imperfectly than not at all. Perhaps you ought to rebuke someone dependent on you, but you are silent for fear of giving way to vehemence; or you avoid the society of certain persons, because they make you cross and impatient. How are you to attain self-control, if you shun all occasions of practicing it? Is not such self-choosing a greater fault than those into which you fear to fall? Aim at a steady mind to do right, go wherever duty calls you, and believe firmly that God will forgive the faults that take our weakness by surprise in spite of our sincere desire to please Him.

JEAN NICOLAS GROU (1731–1803)

For further thought:
1. What is my "SC" (self-control) quotient these days?
2. What can I do to strengthen or undergird that area of my life?

Lord, I have a problem with:

Help me to look to you and:

Let your gentleness be evident to all. The Lord is near. Do not be anxious about anything, but in everything, by prayer and petition, with thanksgiving, present your requests to God.
    —Philippians 4:5, 6, NIV

There are many other ways to look at Paul's admonition here— but there is one aspect of this Pauline command that we usually consider only in connection with other verses. It is simply this: we should not be anxious, because God has a magnificent plan for the lives of each of his children. To discern in some degree the broader outlines of that plan, and to make each day carry us further toward the realization of the goal, is to ally one's life with unconquerable forces. But if we view our life too narrowly, thinking to find the supreme good in immediate circumstances or in present delights and comforts, we miss life's highest end and aim, and we thwart God's gracious purpose for us. To know that my life is fulfilling its divine destiny gives me power to dispense with many frills and to reinterpret all difficulties in the light of God's ultimate triumph— his plan for my life.

For further consideration:
1. Am I living as though "the Lord is near"?
2. What would I be doing differently if I really believed this?

Since "the Lord is near," today I will:

Praise the Lord! Oh give thanks to the Lord, for he is good; for his steadfast love endures for ever!

—Psalm 106:1, RSV

These words, "the Lord is good," occur in some of the most unusual places in the Old Testament. In Nahum 1:7, for example, the prophet says: "The Lord is good, a stronghold in the day of trouble; he knows those who take refuge in him" (RSV). Nahum is predicting the fall of the great city, Nineveh, but at the very beginning of this dire prophecy, he takes time out to recognize that "the Lord is good." No matter what is happening in the world, "the Lord is good"!

This is a comforting thought when I gaze around me and see turmoil running rampant wherever I look. Man is making a real mess of the world God gave him. Every day brings added evidence of his lack of control of the circumstances and events he thought he could handle. But there is One who is in control! He is the One who "is the same yesterday, today, for ever" (Heb. 13:8). Regardless of the chaos and confusion around me, I can rest in that promise and the fact that "the Lord is good."

For further thought:
1. Do I sometimes forget God's goodness and let the world's turmoil wash over me?
2. When this happens, where is the best place to "meet my Maker" and meditate on his goodness?

Lord, today I want to meet you:

Then Moses summoned Joshua, and said to him in the sight of all Israel, "Be strong and of good courage.... It is the Lord who goes before you; he will be with you, he will not fail you or forsake you; do not fear or be dismayed."

—Deuteronomy 31:7, 8, RSV

The words of our text are so important they are repeated in Joshua 1:6, 9. We cannot expect to "cut it" in our day's work or win in our battle with temptation if we approach our tasks with fear and trepidation. To be timid is to be defeated in advance. Yet we must not confuse courage with mere self-assurance. Humility and the sense of dependence upon God's help are not sources of weaknesses but of strength. The secret of victory is to cast all our fear and care upon God and to let his might be our shield and weapon against whatever evil awaits us in the day. As Paul said, "When I am weak, then am I strong" (2 Cor. 12:10). Maltbie D. Babcock wrote:

> Be strong!
> We are not here to play, to dream, to drift,
> We have hard work to do, and loads to lift.
> Shun not the struggle, face it, 'tis God's gift.
> Be strong!

For further reflection:
1. On what or whom do I depend for strength?
2. What was the secret of Joshua's strength (see Joshua 29:15)?

As your servant today, Lord, I will:

Let not your hearts be troubled; believe in God, believe also in me.
—John 14:1, RSV

Of all people on planet earth, Christians have both the right and the privilege to live fearless lives. Our Lord himself is and was a prime example of that kind of living. We Christians should allow our Lord to free us forever from the dread of what each new day might bring—the haunting apprehension of failure or harm that hampers the soul from power-packed living. There is something majestic about the way our Master moved among his peers and amid his circumstances—so unafraid, so steady in his steps, so calm in his attitude toward outward turmoil. He knew that there was nothing to fear because "this is my Father's world." Thus he accepted each day's events as an unfolding of his Father's will, and we can do the same!

For further consideration:
1. What is my usual way of looking at life—calm or fearful?
2. If I am fearful of each day, what positive steps can I take to overcome that fear?

Lord, today I yield to you my fear of:

Scripture Index

Author's Note: Since the pages in this volume are unnumbered, we have used the meditation numbers in the indexes. The system is as follows: each month is numbered (January=1, February=2, March=3, April=4, May=5, June=6, July=7, August=8, September=9, October=10, November=11, and December=12). The number following the solidus (/) refers to the day. Thus 1/1=January 1, 2/2=February 2, etc.

Scripture Index

Scripture Index

Scripture Index

Index of Scripture Readings

Index of Scripture Readings

Index of Scripture Readings

Index of Scripture Readings

Subject Index

Subject Index

Subject Index

Index of Persons and Periodicals Cited

Index of Persons and Periodicals Cited